T0196410

FOOT WASHINGS

DEVOTIONS AND STUDY GUIDES TO BE ABOUT
YOUR FATHER'S BUSINESS

ROGER A. COUTURE

authorHOUSE

AuthorHouse™
1663 Liberty Drive
Bloomington, IN 47403
www.authorhouse.com
Phone: 833-262-8899

Published by AuthorHouse 11/24/2020

ISBN: 978-1-6655-0353-2 (sc)
ISBN: 978-1-6655-0352-5 (e)

Library of Congress Control Number: 2020920037

*My purpose for using various versions of the Bible is to bring clarity and
perspective of the scriptures where I felt it would help to understand.*

*Cover:
Foot Washings Scripture reference John 13:1-17
About Your Father's Business Scripture reference Luke 2:49*

FOREWORD

I have known Roger Couture for many years. Initially he joined a Pastor's Prayer Group that meets weekly to pray for our community and region along the Treasure Coast of Florida. Out of our prayer times together, Roger began attending monthly luncheons for area clergy that I preside over. Later he became a clergy volunteer with the Chapel Ministry I coordinate at the Rock Road Jail which houses 1300 inmates. Roger conducts weekly bible studies in multiple sectors of the facility for some of our hardest to reach inmates. Many of the lessons he taught to our men are an integral part of his book, Foot Washings.

Roger has the gift of teaching. This book is a great discipleship tool to help individuals develop a firm foundation in their walk with Christ. The transformation of our souls if a life long journey. Many believers could benefit from his laborious effort to compile a primer to help ground the reader in the fundamentals of their faith. I found it very informative and instructional. I plan to use it as a manual to help disciple our inmates. I believe his book will help develop substance and character in the lives of all t who read it. His devotions are meticulously developed and reflect a true labor of love for his readers and Jesus.

Dr. David S. Thompson
Senior Staff Chaplain
Saint Lucie County Sheriff's Office
900 Rock Road
Fort Pierce, Fla. 34945
772-462-3437 office
772-318-9093
thompsondav@stluciesheriff.com

DEDICATION

There are many people along my journey with Christ that have inspired, educated, impressed and imparted wisdom, knowledge and teachings to me, and were truly godly witnesses to me. They were friends, pastors, teachers and family. They were young, old and of various backgrounds, races and ethnic groups. The first to tell me about Christ was Sherman Stevens, a coworker. Pastor Bob Phillips who led me to the Lord, Rick and Connie Dodd who invited me into their home for Bible Study and Bishop Rick Callahan who has been a mentor and Pastor, to name a few. Not the least is my wife, Marjorie, who encouraged me (more like "get focused on this project!} and did most of the editing, word processing from start to completion. To her I am most grateful. Most importantly, I am grateful to my Lord and Savior, Jesus Christ, for who He is and all He is in me.

I dedicate this work to those persons who will be saved, transformed, inspired and encouraged as the Holy Spirit guides them in their true calling in life and to those who would use the book to advance the Kingdom of God.

To God be the glory!

Roger A. Couture

Roger A. Couture

PAKISTAN TESTIMONY

(As received)

I am from Pakistan and I am working with Brother Rogers almost a year ago, we are very pleased that God connected us with Brother Rogers, and he has been sending us devotional messages according to our needs, we found that this messages are very meaningful and easy to understand for us, We preached these messages to Muslims and Christian both, many people want to know more about God after listening these devotional message, we invite them in our home prayer meeting and they accept the Lord in their life, we also give them Bible as a gift. I remember one of a church member his name is Suleman, when he came in our prayer meeting for the first time he was arguing a lot about Holy spirit and God, then God gave me wisdom through Brother Rogers message and I preach him and tell the truth and also explain him how God is working in our daily life and even every moment, after visiting us five time he share with me that God change his life he was living a sinful life, taking drug and also very cruel with the wife, but after listening and understanding what God wants from us and we should be obedient to him now I am knowing the true meaning of Christian life, He is very regular to our prayer meetings now and living a blessed life

Ministry name withheld for safety reasons.

CONTENTS

FOREWORD

This special "Foot Washings" devotional guide will help prepare your hearts every day for life's battles and draw you to the Father's heart. Rev. Roger Couture has written some of the best devotions that I have ever read. I love the humor and the quiet strength that comes through the Word of God and Roger's insights and teachings. At the heart of all these writings is the idea that you will be able to pursue your Father's business. Roger has brilliantly woven together devotions and teachings that will build encouragement and strength in your daily walk with Jesus. Reading this challenging book will inspire, educate, and impart wisdom and knowledge into your life and ministry each day. I would like to recommend that you choose to have your own copy of this devotional guide as a welcome friend and faithful companion. Every believer and spiritual leader need a devotional book like this as a watering hole to be refreshed and a place to wash his or her feet with transformation. This book is a resource for all of us who fall in love with Jesus and seek to serve Him with our lives. It is a wealth of spiritual truth that will introduce you to profound insights testifying of the truth. You will be glad you spent time each morning filling your soul with these life-giving messages. Thank you, my dear friends, Rev. Roger & Margie Couture, for sharing this devotional book with me and allowing me the opportunity to encourage others. This is excellent fuel to feed our fire and passion for God. Job well done.

Bishop Richard E Callahan, D.Min., D.D.
Founder and President of Proceeding Word Ministries, Int'l.
Founder and President of Maranatha Ministerial Fellowship, Int'l.

AUTHOR'S PREFACE

Foot Washings is to help you to be about your Father's business. It is a compilation of teachings I have presented to various groups, including Teen Challenge, church pulpits, prisons, homeless shelters and individuals, bible studies and whoever I could gather with.

As Jesus was about His Father's business in (Luke 2:49 MEV, may we be provoked to pursue the Father's will through His Son, Jesus Christ. If doing these devotions leads just one person to become a follower of Christ or lead someone to a closer walk with Him, then I will call this work complete!

Jesus admonished and warned us in Matthew 7:21-23 of the importance of doing the Father's will and the extreme consequences of just being religious.

In some of these devotionals I've used material from other authors, with their permission, and I am thankful for their gifts to the body of Christ. I am also thankful to several people who reviewed the manuscript including Bishop Rick Callahan, Rick and Connie Dodd, Mike Simos and Chaplain Dave Thompson

My purpose in writing this devotional is always to present the Gospel in a format that will lead to practical application by applying spiritual principles in everyday life. Hopefully, this handbook of devotionals will provide the inspiration, education and encouragement to accomplish this.

My hope is that those who read and apply these teachings, will have their heart challenged to change as only the Holy Spirit can. That true transformation will occur and become evidenced in their lives and their joy may be complete.

I sense my words here are inadequate to bring forth what my heart yearns to convey. In that, I can only trust that the Holy Spirit will enlighten you to His glory that He is ready to reveal. I know that "That's how it is with my words. They don't return to me without doing everything I send them to do." Isaiah 55:11 CEV

To God be the glory through His Son Jesus Christ as I go "About My Father's Business".

His servant,

Roger A. Couture

Roger A. Couture
Servant's House Ministries

A.B.C.s OF SALVATION

1 Corinthians 2:10-14 says without God's Spirit one cannot understand His Word, it is all foolishness to them.

Anyone can become a believer in Jesus Christ (Christian) by following the ABCs:

A. Acknowledge your need of a Savior. Luke 2:1

> "for all have sinned and fall short of God's Glory." Romans 3:23 NIV
> And there is salvation in no one else; for there is no other name under heaven that as been given among people by which we must be saved (for God has provided the world no alternative for salvation.) Acts 4:11-12 AMP

B. Believe in Jesus Christ as Savior of your soul and Lord of your Life. John 3:16-17

C. Confess your sins, ask God to forgive you and commit your life to Christ.

> If we claim we have no sin, we are only fooling ourselves and not living in the truth. But if we confess our sins to him, he is faithful and just to forgive us our sins and to cleanse us from all wickedness. If we claim we have not sinned, we are calling God a liar and showing that his word has no place in our hearts. 1 John 1::8-10 NLT

> Someone once told me they tried Christianity and it did not work. It is not something you try but Someone you believe in, Jesus Christ.

How to find verses in the Bible

The Holy Bible contains 66 books: 39 books listed first are called the Old Testament, 27 books that follow are called the New Testament.

Examples; Jeremiah 33:3 is the book Jeremiah chapter 33 and verse 3 is in the Old Testament.

John 3:16 is the book of John chapter 3 and verse 16 in the New Testament.

The book of John is one of the four Gospels which are Matthew, Mark, Luke and John.

The first book in the Old Testament is Genesis, the beginning.

The first book in the New Testament is Matthew.

Some books have more than one and so are numbered as in 2 Timothy 2:3; book of second Timothy, chapter 2 and verse 3.

SECTION 1

NAMES OF GOD

Define His nature and character
Titles used by permission

Dr. Elmer Towne authored a book titled "My Father's Names", about the Old and New Testament names of God to help people know Him more intimately.

I have only used a few of the many names of God from the book. It is worth the time to read and study the many more.

I Am Who I Am
Exodus 3:14 NIV
God said to Moses, "I AM WHO I AM. This is what you are to
say to the Israelites: 'I AM has sent me to you.'"

JEHOVAH ELOHE YESHUATHI-LORD GOD OF MY SALVATION. PSALM 88:1

Jehovah is the Hebrew word for God. Lord is the English translation and first appears in Genesis 2:4, meaning Self-existing one who reveals himself.

God reveals Himself in the New Testament:

A. Christ came to save people from sin. Matthew 1:21

B. Apostle Paul's physical safety from danger at sea is seen in Acts Chapter 27.

C. Of the spiritual and eternal deliverance granted immediately by God to those who accept His conditions of repentance and faith in the Lord Jesus Christ in whom alone it is to be obtained. Acts 4:12

Sozo (Greek) verb; salvation, to guard, keep, preserve from dangers, sickness, with present experiences of God's power to deliver from the bondage of sin.

Some scriptures relating to salvation:

1. Exodus 15:2   Has become my salvation
2. Psalms 51:12   Restore joy of salvation
3. Isaiah 25:9   Trust God for salvation
4. Isaiah 45:17   Israel save everlasting
5. Luke 1:77   Given knowledge of salvation
6. Romans 1:16   Power of God to save
7. Ephesians 6:17   Put on Helmet of salvation
8. Philippians 2:12   Work out salvation with holy fear and trembling
9. Hebrews 2:3   Great salvation
10. Revelations 12:11   Overcome by the blood and testimony of Jesus
11. Roman 8:14   Know that you are children of God.
12. John 3:16   Christ died for you

Memory Verse Acts 4:12 NIV
"Salvation is found in no one else, for there is no other name under heaven given to mankind by which we must be saved"

Rhyme Time
Don't make your vacation
Without God's salvation

Insight:

Some believe in afterlife and some don't. The truth is the Holy Bible gives clear understanding about mankind, this life on Earth and the afterlife.

The Bible is the "Manufacturer's Manual for all People" it clearly defines the way man should live with ourselves and others.

The main purpose of the Bible is to record the history of mankind and his broken relationship with God. To understand the need for a Savior to restore the relationship between man and God and to follow the Bible as a guide written to us on how to live a righteous and holy life while on Earth, while walking, working out our salvation.

> **B**asic
> **I**nstruction
> **B**efore
> **L**eaving
> **E**arth

The neat part is that the Bible teaches that all have a "measure of faith" to believe that Jesus Christ is the Messiah, Savior of the world. Romans 12:3 NKJV

Your Thoughts:

JEHOVAH ROPHE-OUR LORD (OUR) HEALER EXODUS 15:26

Divine healing
Revelation regarding God's Will

4 main ways:

1. God's own pronouncement. Exodus15:26
   Promise of health and healing if they keep His commandments.

2. God's character and nature is the exact representation that Jesus has as Son of God in Hebrews 1:3. Christ's earthly ministry is God's will in action, of healing, miracles and deliverance. In John 6:38, it is in God's heart, nature and purpose to heal all who are sick and oppressed of the devil.

3. The cross of Jesus Christ is the completion of God's plan for all. Matthew 8:16-17. Christ. healed all the sick.

4. Ongoing ministry of the church. Jesus commissioned disciples to heal the sick as part of proclaiming God's Kingdom to them Luke 9:1-6. In Luke 10:1,8-9 Jesus sends out seventy- two men to go to the towns and heal the sick and tell them of the Kingdom of God.

There are three ways recorded in Scripture how God's healing power and faith were imparted (to give a share of):

A. Laying on of hands. Acts 9:17
B. Confession of sin with the laying on of hands, anointing the sick with oil and prayer of faith. James 5:14-16
C. We have been given Spiritual gifts of healing. I Corinthians 12:9

Healing can be hindered by:

1. Unconfessed sins. James 5:16
2. Demonic oppression or bondage sprits Luke 13:11-13
3. Fear or anxiety. Philippians 4:6-7
4. Disappointment undermining faith Mark 5:26
5. People. Mark 10:48
6. Unbiblical teaching. Mark 3:1-5,
7. Doubting heart when you pray. Mark 11:22-24
8. Lack of faith. Mark 6:3-6.
9. Self-centered behavior 1 Corinthians 11:29-30

Why do good people get sick?
Not readily apparent. Galatians 4:13, 1 Timothy 5:23; 2 Timothy 4:20
Other times. 2 Kings 13:14. God will be with you through it all.

What to do for God's divine healing for you??

1. Right relationship with God and others. Matthew 6:33; Also in 1 Corinthians 11:27-30
2. Seek first the presence of Jesus in your life. Romans 12:3; Philippian 2:13
3. If not being healed remain in Christ. John 15:1-7
4. Call for prayer of the elders. James 5:14-16
5. Go to God's people where anointing is present. Acts 5:15-15; 8:5-7.
6. Ask, seek and knock. Matthew 7:8
7. Rejoice always. Philippians 4:4; 11:13.
8. Wait on God for His time and for His work may be displayed. John 9:3
9. God will never leave you nor forsake you. Hebrew 15:5.

The Bible acknowledges proper use of medical care Matthew 9:12; Luke 10:34; Colossians 4:14.

Memory Verse Isaiah 53:5 NIV
But he was pierced for our transgressions,
he was crushed for our iniquities;
the punishment that brought us peace was on him,
by his wounds we are healed.

Rhyme Time
No matter what you feel
Nothing is impossible for God to heal

Insight:

Now comes a subject that can bring much division in the church, that is divine healing for today. Simply said, God's Word identifies Him as the healer, also proclaims that He is not a man that He should lie. He is the same yesterday, today and forever. He is sovereign. (a Person who has Supreme [in God's case] Supernatural powers and Authority), therefore, it becomes His decision how He chooses to heal. I know our job is to pray and believe all of God's Word and promises.

Your Thoughts:

JEHOVAH SHAMMAH- GOD IS THERE

Knowing God's nature and character helps all believers to more clearly understand His way. 1 Kings 8:57 NIV "May the Lord our God be with us as He was with our fathers; may He never leave us or forsake us".

This prayer is answered in the following verses:

Jehovah Shammah "I am the God who is always there" Ever Present God
Ezekiel 48:35 The Lord is there. Also in Matthew 18:20

His word is a commitment to all believers in their struggles with their faith:

a. Joshua 1:5b NIV "I will never leave you nor forsake you". Also in Deuteronomy 31:6
b. Hebrews 13:5 AMP "I will not in any way fail you nor give you up, nor leave you without support, WILL NOT leave you helpless, or let you down, assuredly NOT.
c. Matthew 28:20b NIV "I am with you always to the very end of the age".
d. John 14:16-26 God promises the Holy Spirit to be with us always.
e. John 14:23NKJV He makes our home with Him.
f. Psalms 16:11 AMP In God's presence is fullness of joy.
g. Christ is with you through it all. Acts 18:10

God's answer to all believers concerning; anxiety, trouble, heartache, fear, worry and discouragement is to trust in Him!! Proverbs 3:5-6; Philippians 4:6-7

So....God is always available to you: the Lord is always present
    Through His Word (Bible) reveals Himself
    Through His Holy Spirit convicts us of our sins
    Through prayer (conversing with God, even in dream and visions)
    Through listening for His Spirit

Memory Verse Joshua 1:5 NIV
No one will be able to stand against you all the days of your life.
As I was with Moses, so I will be with you; I will never leave you nor forsake you.

Rhyme Time
He is the God always at my side
Into sin I will not slide

Insight:

With all the communication devices of today, we can be instantly connected with most anyone in the world (assuming they answer right away!). God's Word teaches that He is available 24/7 and He waits for us to connect with Him anytime.

As the scriptures declare in Jeremiah 33:3 AMP call on me and I will answer you and show you great and mighty things, fenced in and hidden, which you do not know (do not distinguish and recognize, have knowledge of or understand).

If God is the first one we seek out with whom to communicate to get Godly wisdom (the comprehensive insight into the ways and purpose of God) why settle for second best from someone else?

Your Thoughts:

JEHOVAH SHALOM-THE LORD OUR PEACE

God granted 40 years of peace to His people, the Hebrews. Judges 6:24 to 8:28

Peace brings rest to our hearts. Sheep lie down by still waters. Psalms 23.

1. God will keep you in perfect peace when your mind is steadfast on Him. Because you trust God. Isaiah 26:3.
2. Psalm 29:11 Lord gives strength and peace to his people.
3. Mercy and truth have meet together, righteousness and peace kiss each other. Psalms 85:10 NIV. There is a godly intimacy with being right with God and having His Peace.
   We are righteous because of the cross of Christ. 1 Corinthians 1:30 and we have the fruit of God's peace given by the Holy Spirit. Galatians 5:22
4. Loving God's law brings great peace. Psalms 119:165
5. Promoter of peace will bring joy. Proverbs 12:20
6. A peaceful heart gives life to the body. Proverbs 14:30
7. Jesus Christ gives us peace to settle our hearts. John 14:27
8. We are Justified through faith we have peace with God through Jesus Christ. Romans 5:1
9. Spirit led thinking brings life and peace. Romans 8:6
10. Kingdom of God is righteousness, peace, joy in Holy Spirit. Romans 14:17.
11. We are admonished by Peter in 1 Peter 3:8-22. This is Peter telling believers how we are to live when we suffer for doing good. This passage is worth reading and meditating on. How we should live as believers. These scriptures are to encourage all of us in the faith that is in Jesus Christ.

Memory Verse Matthew 5:9 KJV
Blessed are the peacemakers,
For they shall be called the children of God

Rhyme Time
To keep your mind at ease
Stay in God's peace

Insight:

History of man has shown that peace is above all a fleeting experience. People, tribes, nations, languages, and leaders, everyone wants peace as they understand it in their own lives and sometimes the lives of others. But it is most always short lived due to problems, such as disease, crises, wars, pestilence and the like. This is because of the fall of man in the Garden of Eden. True peace is only found at the Cross of Christ. What is not hidden from man is that there is One who gives peace because He is the Author of Peace, who is also the Prince of Peace, Jesus Christ. We must rely, turn totally to Christ for His peace. Do not look for substitutes when you can have the real thing.

Since man instinctively won't believe until he sees or tries it, then let us receive Christ and experience His peace! Become a believer of Christ and His Work on the cross for the forgiveness of our sins (erase our sins). Become free to worship Him in spirit and truth. He is the Way, the Truth, and the Life. John 14:6

Yes, let us embrace all the fruits of the Spirit; Love, Joy, Peace, Patience, Goodness, Kindness, Faithfulness, Gentleness and Self-control. All given by the Holy Spirit.

My prayer for you is that your faith in Christ shall increase and the peace of God, which transcends our understanding, will keep your heart and mind on Christ Jesus.

Your Thoughts:

JEHOVAH JIREH -THE LORD WILL PROVIDE GENESIS 22:14

A. Story of Abraham with Isaac about God's providing the sacrifice.
Abraham gives this name of God's provision in Genesis 22:8-14

James 2:21 Abraham considered righteous because of his obedience to God.

God's provision reflected Abraham's faith!

Notice: Abraham did not ask God who would provide the sacrifice!
Abraham said that "God Himself will provide a lamb for the burnt offering" Gen 22:8

B. Testing, suffering, abuse, censured, because of the name of Christ, you are blessed (happy, fortunate, to be envied). 1 Peter 4:12-14
But if you do wrong read Romans 1:18-32, especially verses 18, 21, 22, 23, 26, 28.
In other words, your action will determine your consequences.

God provided food, water, safety to the Israelites in their journeys in the desert for 40 years.

Exodus 15:22, 16: 9-17. God provided meat (Quail) and bread (Manna) for the Hebrews in the desert.

God helps us in all areas of our life!

1. Redemption and salvation for all. John 3:16-17; Ephesians 2:8-9; Psalms 111:9
2. He shows us a way out of temptation.1 Corinthians 10:13
3. God provides everything for our enjoyment. 1 Timothy 6:17-19
4. The Lord's prayer includes all our daily needs. Matthew 6:11
5. God's mercy does not depend on our effort or desire. Romans 9:16
6. God meet your needs according to His riches in Christ. Philippians 4:19

Memory Verse: James 4:10 KJV
Humble yourself in the sight of the Lord
and He shall lift you up

Rhyme Time:
When for Him you decide
He will provide

Insight:

Our culture thrives on self-reliance, independence, do it yourself attitudes. At our best there is much we cannot do on our own. As our Creator, God realizes this and has determined from the beginning that we need His help. When we find out what God is doing and join Him, we will become aware of His provisions in all matters. Jehovah Jireh is our Provider!!!

Let go and let God!

God found Gideon in a hole, Joseph in a prison, He found Daniel in a lion's den.

God has a curious habit of showing up in the midst of trouble, not in the absence.

Where the world sees failure, God sees future.

Next time you feel unqualified to be used by God remember this, He tends to recruit from the pit, not the pedestal. God can and will use anyone, regardless of your status in life to do great works for His glory.

Your thoughts:

2020 VISION

Three types of vision

1. Natural vision is what we see with our eyes.
   We make decisions as to what we see, we are aware of our physical surrounding, wherever we are. Sight is one of the five senses. We correct our vision with glasses and with microscope, telescope, Cat scan and X-ray and other electronic equipment we can see deep inside the physical body and the physical world.

2. Personal vision is how we see our life.
   Either as in Christ, or as we see the world. We have a personal vision for our goals, ourselves, our family, our job, our profession, our calling, our desires and dreams, goals, aspirations etc.

3. Spiritual vision is allowing the Holy Spirit who indwells in us

   (1 Corinthians 6:19) to guide us in all truth.

   John 16:13- 15 NLT

   [13]"When the Spirit of truth comes, he will guide you into all truth. He will not speak on his own but will tell you what he has heard. He will tell you about the future. [14] He will bring me glory by telling you whatever he receives from me. [15] All that belongs to the Father is mine; this is why I said, 'The Spirit will tell you whatever he receives from me." Proverb 29:18

Without guidance from God law and order disappear, but God blesses everyone who obeys his Law.

Some synonyms for vision; · inspiration · intuition · perception · foresight · insight · discernment · awareness ·

Let your revelation (vision) be greater than your situation.
What is your spiritual vision for your future?

I Decree and Declare:

- My neighborhood and community are free from violence and criminal activities and that every evil work is mitigated and destroyed.
- The atmosphere within my community and territory is filled with the Glory of God—an atmosphere conducive for ministries, businesses, agencies, institutions, educational and political systems, relationships, loved ones, tourism, and ideas to thrive.
- My community and territory is characterized by a culture of empowerment.
- The spiritual, economic, social, and political climates shift and take a turn for the best.
- Our land is healed of and free from tornadoes, hurricanes, floods, civil unrest, illegal drugs, human trafficking, pandemic disease, homelessness, illiteracy, gangs, and every evil and demonic work.
- Economic and financial tides are turning in our FAVOR!
- We experience supernatural increase.
- We embrace the true wealth of nations!
- Our communities and territory experience economic growth, restoration, productivity, health and hope.
- The leaders of our communities and territory are moral, ethical, and visionary.
- We as brethren dwell together in unity, celebrating and supporting one another.
- We as responsible citizens continue to lead the charge and raise the bar in fulfilling our spiritual mandates.
- We are the head and not the tail; above only and not beneath; first and not last.
- We live a humble life of gratitude and thanksgiving knowing that He who has begun this good work will complete it!

Written by Apostle Trevor Banks used by permission. Regarding "I Decree and Declare": This is read each time a group of 20 Christian pastors, ministers and civic leaders come together for weekly prayer. We have been meeting since January, 2015. The prayer emphasis is for our cities, communities, region and nation to have on influence on the" Seven Mountains": Media, Government, Education, Entertainment, Economy, Religion and Family. We have seen gains in some of these areas, "the earnest prayer of a righteous person has great power and produces wonderful results". James 5:16 NLT   PRAISE THE LORD!

SECTION 2

YOUR IDENTITY IN CHRIST

The Bible shows many references to our identity as believers in Jesus Christ. I have defined some of the forty-eight references I have found.

CHRIST'S UNIQUENESS

NKJV Unless specified

"Who do you say I Am?"
This is a most important question Jesus asked. Matthew 16:13-17
Do you believe He is the Christ (Messiah)?

> 13 When Jesus came to the region of Caesars Philippi, He asked His disciples, "Who do people say the Son of Man is?" 14 They replied, "Some say John the Baptist, others say Elijah; and still others, Jeremiah or on of the prophets" 15"But what about you?" He asked. "Who do you say I am?" 16 Simon Peter answered, You are the Christ, the Son of the living God". 17 Jesus replied, "Blessed are you, Simon Son of Jonah, for this was not revealed to you by man, but by my Father in Heaven."

I found 365 prophecies of the Messiah (Christ) in 27 of the 39 books of the Old Testament that were fulfilled in New Testament and written between 1450 BC and 400 BC.

Prophecy is described as a prediction of the future, or a revelation of God.

These are some of the prophecies:

Prophecies;	Found in;	Fulfilled in;
1. Offering of women	Genesis 3:15	Galatians 4:4
2. Place of birth	Micah 5:2	Matthew 2:1
3. Virgin birth	Isaiah 7:14	Matthew 1:14
4. As a Prophet	Deuteronomy18:15	John 6:14
5. Falsely accused	Psalms 27;12	Matthew 26:60
6. Crucified	Isaiah 52:12	Matthew 27:38
7. Resurrection	Psalm 16:10	Matthew 28:9
8. Ascension	Psalm 68:19	Luke 24:50-51

Why should you believe? Because of the abundance of evidence with.

So, what is your reason for not believing? Here are some reasons people make for not accepting Christ, followed by some scriptures to encourage you to in making a decision to follow Christ.

   a. Can't do it now!
       Joshua 24:15 NIV "Choose this day who you will serve"

   b. Too late for me.
       Romans 10:13 NLT "everyone who calls on the name of the Lord will be saved".

c. Tried it.
   Philippians 4:13 NLT "I can do everything through Christ who gives me strength".

d. Don't understand.
   John 13:7 NIV Jesus replied, "You do not realize now what I am doing, but later you will understand.

e. I'm okay.
   John 3:36b NIV "Whoever rejects the Son will not see life, for God's wrath remains in them".

f. God loves everybody.
   Galatians 6:7 NIV "Do not be deceived, God is not mocked; for whatever a man sows, that he will also reap".

g. Hypocrites in the church.
   Romans 14:12 NLV Every one of us will give an answer to God about himself.

h. I can't afford the tithe or time.
   Mark 8:36 "For what will it profit a man if he gains the whole world, and loses his own soul?

i. I don't want to leave my old friends,
   1 Cor. 15:33 NIV "Do not be misled, bad company corrupts good character".

j. People will hate me.
   Matthew 5:11 There is a blessing connected to it.

Memory Verse Hebrews 13:8
Jesus Christ *is* the same yesterday, today, and forever.

Rhyme Time
Some then and now call Him a liar,
Does not change that He is the Messiah.

Insight:

Not only has Jesus Christ affected people like no other in history, He continues to cause the hearts of people to be transformed according to God's Will.

People seek religion (finding a god). True religion is having a personal relationship with Jesus Christ, the Savior of the world.

Being a Christian is not something we try to see if it works for us, it is some ONE we believe in, Jesus Christ.

Your Thoughts:

I AM A CHOSEN PEOPLE

Scriptures are NKJV unless noted otherwise

Chosen ones, Royal Priesthood, Holy Nation, Special People, Proclaim His praises.

1 Peter 2:9
"But you *are* a chosen generation, a royal priesthood, a holy nation, His own special people, that you may proclaim the praises of Him who called you out of darkness into His marvelous light".

   A. Chosen generation (people) Ephesians 1:4
      "just as He chose us in Him before the foundation of the world, that we should be holy and without blame before Him in love".

      Also found in Psalm 4:3, John 15:16, James 2:5

   B. Royal priesthood. 1 Peter 2:5
      "you also, as living stones, are being built up a spiritual house, a holy priesthood, to offer up spiritual sacrifices acceptable to God through Jesus Christ".

      Also found in Exodus 19:6, Isaiah 61:6, Rev 1:4-6, Rev 20:6

   C. Holy Nation (people). 1 Thessalonians 3:13
      "so that He may establish your hearts blameless in holiness before our God and Father at the coming of our Lord Jesus Christ with all His saint".

      Also found in Isiah 35:8, Heb 12:10. 1 Peter 2:5,9 Rev. 21:3

   D. Special People, (Belonging to God) Ephesians 2:19
      "Consequently, you are no longer foreigners and strangers, but fellow citizens with God's people and also members of his household".

   E. Proclaim His praise. Psalm 66:8
      "Oh, bless our God, you peoples! And make the voice of His praise to be heard".

      Also found in Psalms 145-150

Memory Verse Acts 7:50
Has not my hand made all these things?

Rhyme Time

Man's inheritance is temporal

God's inheritance is eternal

Insights:

This is our inheritance in Christ, as believers we are the heirs of all He has for us. Most inheritances that people receive are the result of someone's death. Our inheritance from God is now Jesus Christ who died on the cross and rose from the dead and is alive so that we may believe in Christ and inherit eternal life.

Your Thoughts:

I HAVE FREEDOM IN CHRIST

Scriptures are (NKJV) unless noted otherwise

1. I AM FREE FROM THE LAW OF SIN AND DEATH.

Romans 8:1-2
1 There is therefore now no condemnation to those who are in Christ Jesus, who do not walk according to the flesh, but according to the Spirit. 2 For the law of the Spirit of life in Christ Jesus has made me FREE from the law of sin and death

Free (freedom) DEFINED:
>   Not under the control or in the power of another
>   No condemnation, guiltless
>   boundless
>   Liberty
>   Autonomy (making your own choices)
>   Clear of obstruction and obstacles
>   No bondage
>   No slavery
>   No hindrance
>   Free choice
>   Unimpeded
>   Released from captivity of thoughts and attitudes contrary to God's word.

2. WHAT DOES IT MEAN TO HAVE FREEDOM IN CHRIST?

The Holy Spirit in us through Jesus Christ, set us spiritually free from any and all evil and/or human spirit(s) that would hinder, stop, block, obstruct, distract, or by any other means keep us from worshiping God. We are set FREE to worship God!

Romans 6:10
For the death He died, He died to sin once for all, but the life that He lives, He lives for God. It is a Spiritual principle in the Word of God, the Bible, that Christ's death on the cross overcame the power of sin in the world.

1 John 5:4-5
4.For whatever is born of God overcomes the world. And this is the victory that has overcome the world—our faith. 5 Who is he who overcomes the world, but he who believes that Jesus is the Son of God?

John 16:33 These things I have spoken to you, that in Me you may have peace. In the world you will have tribulation; but be of good cheer, I have overcome the world. This freedom empowered by the Holy Spirit in us is the result of Christ's sacrifice on the cross. When we believe and accept this perfect sacrifice in our heart, we now have the Holy Spirit in us with all His power to overcome and resist any and all temptation which lead to sin.

3. OUR RESPONSE;

   A. LIVE IN CHRIST.
     John 8:31-32
     then Jesus said to those Jews who believed Him, "If you abide in My word, you are My disciples indeed. 32 And you shall know the truth, and the truth shall make you free.

     Galatians 2:20
     I have been crucified with Christ; it is no longer I who live, but Christ lives in me; and the *life* which I now live in the flesh I live by faith in the Son of God, who loved me and gave Himself for me.

   B. *P.R.A.Y.*
     <u>P</u>repare your heart by humbly repenting of your sins.
       <u>R</u>evere Him, He is worthy of all praise.
         <u>A</u>ccept his word for you. In your prayer take time to listen.
           <u>Y</u>ield your life to the Holy Spirit in you.

     Rejoicing in hope, patient in tribulation, continuing steadfastly in prayer. Romans 12:12

   C. BE A GOD SEEKER.
     Matthew 6:33
     But seek first the kingdom of God and His righteousness, and all these things shall be added to you.

Memory Verse John 8:32 ERV
Then you will know the truth, and the truth will set you free.

Rhyme Time
The person who is free
in Christ can always be.

Insight:

Salvation is the key to becoming free and receive all God has for us.

Then we are to continue being transformed in all areas of our life. Romans 12:1-2

God provides all His blessings, it is up to us to receive them, apply them in our lives for His glory to bless others.

Your thoughts:

POWER AND BLESSINGS

A. Power over oppression and fear.

    Isaiah 54:14-17 (NKJV)

14 In righteousness you shall be established;
You shall be far from oppression, for you shall not fear;
And from terror, for it shall not come near you.
15 Indeed they shall surely assemble, *but* not because of Me.
Whoever assembles against you shall fall for your sake.
16 "Behold, I have created the blacksmith
Who blows the coals in the fire,
Who brings forth an instrument for his work;
And I have created the spoiler to destroy.
17 No weapon formed against you shall prosper,
And every tongue *which* rises against you in judgment You shall condemn. his
is the heritage of the servants of the Lord,
Also found in Psalms 34:7, Psalm 91:4, Luke 21:18

B. Five levels of attack from the enemy;

1. Impress; *to affect deeply or* strongly in mind or feelings; influence in opinion:
2. Depress; *to make sad* or gloomy; lower in spirits; deject; dispirit.
3. Oppress; *to lie heavily upon* (the mind, a person, etc.)
   From Hebrew (ravage, to be burly, powerful, is strong, beefy, hefty, brawny)

4. 4. Obsess; t*o dominate* or preoccupy the thoughts,
   feelings, or desires of (a person); beset, trouble, or haunt persistently or abnormally:

5. Possess; *to have* as belonging to one; have; as property; own: at this stage possessions
   can lead you to harmful actions, even suicide.

C. Blessings

    Holy and without blame Ephesians 1:3-5 NKJV
3 Blessed *be* the God and Father of our Lord Jesus Christ, who has blessed
us with every spiritual blessing in the heavenly *places* in Christ, 4 just as He
chose us in Him before the foundation of the world, that we should be holy
and without blame before Him in love, 5 having predestined us to adoption as
sons by Jesus Christ to Himself, according to the good pleasure of His will,

    Also in 1 Peter 1:12-16

Memory Verse John 10:10 AMP
The thief comes only to steal and kill and destroy;
I have come that they may have life, and have it to the full

Rhyme Time
Be Christ's possession
It will keep you from evil oppression

Insight:

What does it mean to "have life to the full? In John 10:10. The answer is an experiential one. For each of us must seek this personally, my experience in fullness of life in Christ is but a testimony to you. It has been said if you take care of God's business, God will take care of your business.

Your thoughts:

NEW CREATION, RECONCILED TO GOD, AMBASSADOR OF GOD, AND MADE RIGHTEOUS

A. New creation 2 Corinthians 5:17 (NLT)

17 This means that anyone who belongs to Christ has become a new person. The old life is gone; a new life has begun

Also Mark 10:6, John 3:3, 16 3:17, Gen 1:27, Galatians 6:15, 1 Peter 1:20

B. Message of reconciliation

Matthew 5:23-24 ERV

23 So if you are about to offer your <u>gift</u> to God at the altar and there you remember that your brother has something against you, 24 leave your gift there in front of the altar, go at once and make peace with your brother, and then come back and offer your gift to God.

Also in Romans 5:10, Col 1:20

C. Ambassador

Ephesians 6:20 NET

20 I am in chains now, still preaching this message as God's ambassador. So pray that I will keep on speaking boldly for him, as I should.

D. Righteousness of God Psalm 5:12 NLT

12 For you bless the godly, O Lord;
you surround them with your shield of love. Also Proverbs 33:3, Proverbs 10,11,12

These are connected together in this text.

2 Corinthians 5:16-21 NLT

16 So we have stopped evaluating others from a human point of view. At one time we thought of Christ merely from a human point of view. How differently we know him now! 17 This means that anyone who belongs to Christ has become a new person. The old life is gone; a new life has begun! 18 And all of this is a gift from God, who brought us back to himself through Christ. And God has given us this task of reconciling people to him. 19 For God was in Christ, reconciling the world to himself, no longer counting people's sins against them. And he gave us this wonderful message of reconciliation. 20 So we are Christ's ambassadors; God is making his appeal through us. We speak for Christ when we plead, "Come back to God!" 21 For God made Christ, who never sinned, to be the offering for our sin so that we could be made right with God through Christ.

Memory Verse 2 Corinthians 5:17 NKJV
Therefore, if anyone *is* in Christ, *he is* a new creation;
old things have passed away; behold, all things have become new.

Rhyme Time
A Christian life
will bring less strife

Insight:

Now is the time to be involved with those assignments as an ambassador for Christ. Already having attained the prerequisite of a new creation and reconciled to God through His Son Jesus Christ and being in right standing (righteous) with God.

Your Thoughts:

CHRIST IN ME

Submitted to God
Given power

A. Life in Christ
    Galatians 2:19-20 NIV
    19 For I through the law died to the law that I might live to God. 20 I have been crucified with Christ; it is no longer I who live, but Christ lives in me; and the *life* which I now live in the flesh I live by faith in the Son of God, who loved me and gave Himself for me.

    Also in Galatians 2:20, Luke 20:38, Romans 6:11, Romans 14:8

B. Submit to God;
    James 4:7 NKJV
    Therefore submit to God. Resist the devil and he will flee from you.
    Matthew 6:10, Matthew 26:39, Romans 6:13, James 4:1-10, 2Corinthians 5:15

C. Power Given:
    2 Timothy 1:7 NKJV
    For God has not given us a spirit of fear, but of power and of love and of a sound mind.

    Not given F.E.A.R.
    False Evidence Appearing Real
    Finding Excuses And Reasons
    Fear Expected Against Reason

    Instead:
    Face Everything And Rejoice
    Face Everything And Rise
    Face Evil And Rebuke

    Holy Spirit Power:
    Zechariah 4:6 (All power from Holy Spirit), Matthew 3:11 (Baptized with Holy Spirit anointing). Acts 4:31-33 (prayed together, great power provided), Ephesians 3:16 (Prayer brings Holy Spirit power and superabundant works vs 20) Colossians 1:9-12 (prayer to strenghten with all power).

D. Sound Mind-
    1 Corinthians 2:15-16. Mind of Christ.
    Synonym; Sane, rational, to detect with senses, spiritually discerning, distinguish, recognize

Memory Verse Matthew 28:18 NLV
Jesus came and said to them,
"All power has been given to Me in heaven and on earth."

Rhyme Time
God is your strong tower
To overcome in His power

Insight:

The main role of our DNA molecules is the long-term storage of information. In having God's "spiritual DNA", as you are the temple of the Holy Spirit, you have all information readily available to you. No one can steal or destroy your identity in Christ, for you have God's DNA! You have a sound mind. John 16:13 NLT says "But when he, the Spirit of truth, comes, he will guide you into all truth. For he will not speak on his own authority, but will speak whatever he hears, and will tell you what is to come".

Your Thoughts:

POSITION, POWER, PURPOSE AND POSSIBILITIES

These scriptures show how we can experience the above.
Complete means nothing is lacking (all, fullness, intact).

Colossians 2:8-10 NLT
Don't let anyone capture you with empty philosophies and high-sounding nonsense that come from human thinking and from the spiritual power of this world, rather than from Christ. 9 For in Christ lives all the fullness of God in a human body. 10 So you also are complete through your union with Christ, who is the head over every ruler and authority.

James 1:4 NIV
Let perseverance finish its work so that you may be mature and complete, not lacking anything.

John 15:9-11 verse 11 NIV
I have told you this so that my joy may be in you and that your joy may be complete.

John 17:22-23 NIV
I have given them the glory that you gave me, that they may be one as we are one— 23 I in them and you in me—so that they may be brought to complete unity. Then the world will know that you sent me and have loved them even as you have loved me.

Unlike human wills that determine who receives the inheritance, God provides all the inheritance of his Kingdom while we are still alive. There is no contesting His will with anyone as so many do in our courts today.

As heirs of God and co-heirs with Christ our position is clearly established.

1. Position:

    I am a child of God,
    John 1:12
    As a believer in Jesus Christ, Savior and Lord.

    John 3:16
    I am born again of the Spirit of God.

    All I need will be provided by Almighty God, Creator of all things visible and invisible All His promises and blessings are yes in Christ's name.

Romans 8:17 NIV

Now if we are children, then we are heirs—heirs of God and co-heirs with Christ, if indeed we share in his sufferings in order that we may also share in his glory.

Acts 3:24-26 NIV verse 25 And you are heirs of the prophets and of the covenant God made with your fathers. He said to Abraham, 'Through your offspring all peoples on earth will be blessed.

James 1:9 NIV

Believers in humble circumstances ought to take pride in their high position.

2. Power:

The supernatural power of the Holy Spirit living in me to accomplish all the work He has appointed me to do. Ephesians 6:10 (paraphrase)

1 John 4:4 NIV

You, dear children, are from God and have overcome them, because the one who is in you is greater than the one who is in the world.

Acts 1:8 NLV

But you will receive power when the Holy Spirit comes on you; and you will be my witnesses in Jerusalem, and in all Judea and Samaria, and to the ends of the earth."

Job 27:10-11 NIV

Will they find delight in the Almighty?
Will they call on God at all times?
"I will teach you about the power of God;
the ways of the Almighty I will not conceal."

3. Purpose:

To be about the Fathers business. Luke 2:49 NKJV and He said to them, "Why did you seek Me? Did you not know that I must be about My Father's business?"

Our business is being about His business!

4. Possibilities:

Ephesians 3:20 NLV God is able to do much more than we ask or think through His power working in us.

With God all things are possible. Nothing is impossible. Mark 10:27.

Memory Verse Mark 9:23 MEV
Jesus said to him, "If you can believe, all things *are* possible to him who believes."

Rhyme Time
You will be thrilled
In doing God's will

Insight:

All of these; position, power, purpose and possibilities in your life are already destined to you in God's Word. Jeremiah 29:11 NKJV For I know the thoughts that I think toward you, says the Lord, thoughts of peace and not of evil, to give you a future and a hope. Stop searching and begin working in the Kingdom. Benefits are eternal!

Your thoughts:

YOU ARE A WORKER ENGAGED BY GOD

Ephesians 2:8-9 NKJV First, you are saved by grace through faith.
8 For by grace you have been saved through faith, and that not of yourselves; *it is* the gift of God, **9** not of works, lest anyone should boast.

Now the good works He has for you to do you are empowered by the Holy Spirit for His purpose.

Four different bible version say the same with different words regarding work.

A. Ephesians 2:10 NKJV
   10 For we are his workmanship, created in Christ Jesus unto good works, which God +hath before ordained that we should walk in them. Works: From Greek poy-ay-mah thing that is made, product, productive.
B. Ephesians 2:10 AMP 10 handiwork (His workmanship), good works
C. Ephesians 2:10 NLT 10 For we are God's masterpiece. To do good things.
D. Ephesians 2:10 NLV His work. work for Him.

Good works unto God requires;

Honesty, Integrity, Faithfulness, Commitment, Selflessness, Humbleness, Praising God
Your faith will produce good work.
James 2:26 NKJV as the body without the spirit is dead, so faith without works is dead.
Read James 2:14-26
Many Old and New Testament scriptures refer to God's workers
Moses, Jacob Joseph, David, Solomon, the prophets speaking God's word.
All workers in God's Kingdom.
Romans 16:3   Priscilla and Aguila
Romans 16:21   Timothy
2 Corinthians 8:23 Titus
Colossians 4:11 Justus and the list goes on....

Become a worker approved by God.

2 Timothy 2:15-16 NLT
Work hard so you can present yourself to God and receive his approval. Be a good worker, one who does not need to be ashamed and who correctly explains the word of truth. [16] Avoid worthless, foolish talk that only leads to more godless behavior.

Godless behavior is lack of fairness or justice, discrimination, favoritism, hatred, intolerance, prejudice, wrong, partial, evil.

Matthew 9:37 NLT
He said to His disciples "the harvest is great but the workers are few".

Colossians 3:23 NIV
Whatever you do, work at it with all your heart, as working for the Lord, not for human masters,

Memory Verse 1 Corinthians 3:9 NIV
For we are co-workers in God's service; you are God's field, God's building.

Rhyme Time
All the work you are given
Your reward is in heaven

Insight:

This identity in Christ is completely opposite of the worldly mind set. In essence we are to work our best in all manner, this will be to many, a witness of Christ in our lives and bring glory to God. Your calling in life is to do good works in Christ. Your wages are in this life and the life to come.

What business (work) for God are you doing?

Your thoughts:

A.L.I.V.E

All Living In Victory Everyday

A. I AM ALIVE IN CHRIST
Ephesians 2 1-9 (NIV)

1 As for you, you were dead in your transgressions and sins, 2 in which you used to live when you followed the ways of this world and of the ruler of the kingdom of the air, the spirit who is it now at work in those who are disobedient. 3 All of us also lived among them at one time, gratifying the cravings of our flesh[] and following its desires and thoughts. Like the rest, we were by nature deserving of wrath. 4 But because of his great love for us, God, who is rich in mercy, 5 made us alive with Christ even when we were dead in transgressions—it is by grace you have been saved. 6 And God raised us up with Christ and seated us with him in the heavenly realms in Christ Jesus, 7 in order that in the coming ages he might show the incomparable riches of his grace, expressed in his kindness to us in Christ Jesus. 8 For it is by grace you have been saved, through faith—and this is not from yourselves, it is the gift of God — 9 not by works, so that no one can boast. 10 For we are God's handiwork, created in Christ Jesus to do good works, which God prepared in advance for us to do.

B. I AM FREE OF GUILT
Romans 8:1-8 (NIV)

Therefore, there is now no condemnation for those who are in Christ Jesus, 2 because through Christ Jesus the law of the Spirit who gives life has set you [a] free from the law of sin and death. 3 For what the law was powerless to do because it was weakened by the flesh, [a] God did by sending his own Son in the likeness of sinful flesh to be a sin offering. []And so he condemned sin in the flesh, 4 in order that the righteous requirement of the law might be fully met in us, who do not live according to the flesh but according to the Spirit.

5 Those who live according to the flesh have their minds set on what the flesh desires; but those who live in accordance with the Spirit have their minds set on what the Spirit desires. 6 The mind governed by the flesh is death, but the mind governed by the Spirit is life and peace. 7 The mind governed by the flesh is hostile to God; it does not submit to God's law, nor can it do so. 8 Those who are in the realm of the flesh cannot please God.

C. I HAVE POWER OVER SIN
1 John 5:18-20 NIV

We know that anyone born of God does not continue to sin; the One who was born of God keeps them safe, and the evil one cannot harm them. 19 We know that we are children of God, and that the whole world is under the control of the evil one. 20 We know also that the Son of God has come and has given us understanding, so that we may know him who is true. And we are in him who is true by being in his Son Jesus Christ. He is the true God and eternal life.

D. I AM BLESSED

EPHESIANS 1:3-5 (NIV)

3 Praise be to the God and Father of our Lord Jesus Christ, who has blessed US in the heavenly realms with every spiritual blessing in Christ.4 For he chose us in him before the creation of the world to be holy and blameless in his sight. In love 5 he[b] predestined us for adoption to son ship[c] through Jesus Christ, in accordance with his pleasure and will.

E. I AM CALLED TO BE HOLY

1 Peter 1:13-16 NIV

13 Therefore, with minds that are alert and fully sober, set your hope on the grace to be brought to you when Jesus Christ is revealed at his coming. 14 As obedient children, do not conform to the evil desires you had when you lived in ignorance. 15 But just as he who called you is holy, so be holy in all you do; 16 for it is written; "Be holy, because I am holy."!

F. I HAVE THE MIND of CHRIST

1 Corinthians 2:9-16 MEV

9 However, as it is written: "What no eye has seen, what no ear has heard, and what no human mind has conceived, the things God has prepared for those who love Him. 10 these are things God has revealed to us by His Spirit. The Spirit searches all things, even the deep things of God. 11 For who knows a person's thoughts except their own spirit within them? In the same way no one knows the thoughts of God except the Spirit of God. 12 What we have received is not the spirit of the world, but the Spirit who is from God, so that we may understand what God has freely given us. 13 This is what we speak, not in words taught us by human wisdom but in words taught by the Spirit, explaining spiritual realities with Spirit-taught words. 14 The person without the Spirit does not accept the things that come from the Spirit of God but considers them foolishness, and cannot understand them because they are discerned only through the Spirit. 15 The person with the Spirit makes judgments about all things, but such a person is not subject to merely human judgments, 16 for, "Who has known the mind of the Lord so as to instruct him?" But we have the mind of Christ.

ALSO found in

Philippians 2:1-4 New International Version NIV

1 Therefore if you have any encouragement from being united with Christ, if any comfort from his love, if any common sharing in the Spirit, if any tenderness and compassion, 2 then make my joy complete by being like-minded, having the same love, being one in spirit and of one mind. 3 Do nothing out of selfish ambition or vain conceit. Rather, in

humility value others above yourselves, 4 not looking to your own interests but each of you to the interests of the others.

G. I HAVE THE PEACE OF GOD
Philippians 4:4-7 ESV
4 Rejoice in the Lord always. I will say it again: Rejoice!
5 Let your gentleness be evident to all. The Lord is near. Do not be anxious about anything, but in every situation, by prayer and petition, with thanksgiving, present your requests to God 7 And the peace of God, which transcends all understanding, will guard your hearts and your minds in Christ Jesus.

Memory verse: Galatians 2:20 (NIV)
I have been crucified with Christ and I no longer live, but Christ lives in me. The life I now live in the body, I live by faith in the Son of God, who loved me and gave himself for me.

Rhyme Time:
The world is at odds
With those who are in God

Insight:

Life is 10% what happens to you and 90% how you react to it. Our understanding of scripture is extremely important. We need to live in Christ as defined in all the ways God shows us in the Bible. In this day and age scrutiny of who someone is can become a security issue. You are all of these in Jesus Christ; alive, free from guilt, have power over sin, have spiritual blessing, called to be holy, have mind of Christ and have God's peace.

You have it all! What will you do with it.

Your Thoughts:

VOICE OF HIS PRAISE

Praise is glorify, worship, applaud, acclaim, hail, salute, exalt, devotion, thanks, laud. I found 144 praise verses from Exodus to Revelation.

Christians often speak of "praising God," and the Bible commands all living creatures to praise the Lord (Psalm 150:6).

One Hebrew word for "praise" is **yadah**, meaning "praise, give thanks, or confess." extending the hand vigorously.

A second word often translated "praise" in the Old Testament is **zamar,** "sing praise." to touch the strings, mostly rejoicing.

A third word translated "praise" is **halal** (the root of *hallelujah*), meaning "to praise, honor, or commend." to boast, to rave, celebrate.

All three terms contain the idea of giving thanks and honor to One who is worthy of praise.

Some foundation scriptures of praise are in Psalm 63:4, 100:4, 134:2, 1 Timothy 2:8. Psalm 66:8 Oh, bless our God, you peoples! And make the voice of His praise to be heard,

Psalm 22:23 NKJV You who fear the Lord, praise Him! All you descendants of Jacob, glorify Him, And fear Him, all you offspring of Israel! Psalm 43:5 Why are you cast down, O my soul? And why are you disquieted within me? Hope in God; For I shall yet praise Him, The help of my countenance and my God.

Psalm 107:32 NKJV Let them exalt Him also in the assembly of the people, And praise Him in the company of the elders.

Psalm 150 uses the term praise thirteen times in six verses. The first verse provides the **"where"** of praise—everywhere! "Praise God in his sanctuary; praise him in his mighty heavens (open skies)

The next verse teaches **"why"** to praise the Lord: "Praise him for his acts of power; praise him for his surpassing greatness."

Verses 3–6 note **"how"** to praise the Lord—with a variety of instruments, dance, and everything that has breath. Every means we have to make sound is to be used to praise the Lord

We are reminded **"When"** to praise God:

In Psalm 34, David reminds us that we should praise God through the good times and bad. Praise should fill our hearts every day, no matter our circumstances – especially when we are walking through seasons of great trials.

A Vocation of Praise. Praising God is a God-appointed calling. Indeed, God has formed for himself a people "that they may proclaim my [God's] praise" (Isa 43:21)
Praise is both a duty and a delight of which is the unique nature of God (1 Chron 29:10-13).

Some Biblical Expressions of Praise
Declaring of thanks (Heb. 13:15) Clapping hands and shouting (Psalms 47:1) Musical instruments and dancing 150:4) Singing praise songs (Psalms 9:11)

Psalms, hymns, & spiritual songs (Ephesians 5:19-20)

Making a joyful noise (Psalms 98:4) By lifting our hands (Psalms 134:2)
By being still (Psalms 4:3-5, 46:10)
By being loud (Psalms 33:3, 95:1-6)

ALSO:
1. Fruit of our lips. Isaiah. 57:19
   Praise continually. Heb 13:15

2. God perfects our praise. Matt. 21:16
   Praising with the Word. Col. 3:16
   Praising in the Spirit. Ephesians 5:19 (17-19)

3. Strength in praise to silence the enemy and the avenger Psalm 8:2
   Offer thanksgiving, call him in trouble,
   praise him, stay right, receive his salvation Psalm 50:14,15,23
   Praise puts us into God's will1 Thessalonians 5:16-18
   Praise with all our heart, enemies will be turned away Psalm 9:1-4

Memory Verse Nehemiah 9:5b
Stand up and praise the Lord your God
Who is from everlasting to everlasting

Rhyme Time
God reveals his power
As we praise Him every hour

Insight:

We all have the power of praise in us. With our voices we can magnify the Lord anytime, anywhere! In doing so we release supernatural (Holy Spirit) power. We are the voice of His praise! He inhabits the praises of His people Psalm 22:3 KJV

"It is the same with my word. I send it out, and it always produces fruit.
It will accomplish all I want it to, and it will prosper everywhere I send it." Isaiah 55:11 NLT

Prosper synonyms: do well, flourish, multiply, thrive, blossom.
When the praises go up the blessings come down

Your thoughts:

QUOTES

"The things you trust in your mind
Will occupy your time."
unknown

In every great aspect of life
you can apply God's Word.
R, Couture

No Jesus, no Word
Know Jesus, Know Word
unknown

"We make a living by what we get
We make a life by what we give."
Winston Churchill

Lawyers use legal voice,
Doctors use medical voice,
Bankers use financial voice,
Believers use the voice of His praise.
R. Couture

Mind in the beginning
What matters most in the end
Unknown

F.A.I.T.H Word
Faith As In The Holy Word
Faith As In The Healing Word
R. Couture

SECTION 3

LIFE GUIDING DEVOTIONS

To help you be "About the Father's Business"

LOOK WHAT THE LORD HAS DONE

Let us consider how we can apply the word HOPE in your life.

Humble yourself in the sight of the Lord and He will lift you up. James 4:10
   Obey God's Commandments. John 14:15
      Pray & Praise Him in all circumstances. 1 Thessalonians 5:16-18
         Everyday decide to practice the above.

Living in this world today, will we let fear and anxiety rule our lives or will we trust and hope in God? Christ promises to give you His peace as we read in John 14:27. Proverbs 3:5-8 says to trust God in all things and He will guide your life. God says in Hebrews 13:5b, that He will never leave you nor forsake you. The choice is yours to make daily.

Begin to trade this for that:
    Trade fear for faith.
    Trade anxiety for Almighty
    Trade hopelessness for healing
    Trade panic for peace
    Trade nervousness for new life
    Trade depression for deliverance
    Trade stress for surrender
    Trade uncertainty for unconditional love

A. Let us review what God has already given believers in Jesus Christ.
The Armor of God, Ephesian 6:10-18 ESV. 10 Finally, be strong in the Lord and in his mighty power.[11] Put on the full armor of God, so that you can take your stand against the devil's schemes. [12] For our struggle is not against flesh and blood, but against the rulers, against the authorities, against the powers of this dark world and against the spiritual forces of evil in the heavenly realms.[13] Therefore put on the full armor of God, so that when the day of evil comes, you may be able to stand your ground, and after you have done everything, to stand.[14] Stand firm then, with the belt of truth buckled around your waist, with the breastplate of righteousness in place,[15] and with your feet fitted with the readiness that comes from the gospel of peace.[16] In addition to all this, take up the shield of faith, with which you can extinguish all the flaming arrows of the evil one. [17] Take the helmet of salvation and the sword of the Spirit, which is the word of God.[18] And pray in the Spirit on all occasions with all kinds of prayers and requests. With this in mind, be alert and always keep on praying for all the Lord's people.

In vs 17 the sword of the Spirit, which is the word of God, is our offensive weapon. All the others are protective in nature. All the armor of God is to remain on you!

The Apostle Paul used the protective body equipment of the soldiers of his day as a parallel example of the spiritual protection we have, as Christians, for our mind, our spirit and our soul. Understand that this armor is impossible to break through because it is powered by the Holy Spirit.

B. Live by the Spirit / Let the fruit of the Spirit grow in you and become your characteristic as a person, as a believer.
Galatians 5:22-26 ESV But the fruit of the Spirit is love, joy, peace, forbearance, kindness, goodness, faithfulness,[23] gentleness and self-control. Against such things there is no law. [24] Those who belong to Christ Jesus have crucified the flesh with its passions and desires.[25] Since we live by the Spirit, let us keep in step with the Spirit [26] Let us not become conceited, provoking and envying each other.

C. God works through the spiritual gifts he gives to believers.
1 Corinthians 12:1-11 NIV Also found in Chapter 14

Concerning spiritual gifts:
1 Now about the gifts of the Spirit, brothers and sisters, I do not want you to be uninformed.2 You know that when you were pagans, somehow or other you were influenced and led astray to mute idols.3 Therefore I want you to know that no one who is speaking by the Spirit of God says, "Jesus be cursed," and no one can say, "Jesus is Lord," except by the Holy Spirit. 4 There are different kinds of gifts, but the same Spirit distributes them. 5There are different kinds of service, but the same Lord. There are different kinds of working, but in all of them and in everyone it is the same God at work. 7 Now to each one the manifestation of the Spirit is given for the common good.8To one there is given through the Spirit a message of wisdom, to another a message of knowledge by means of the same Spirit,9 to another faith by the same Spirit, to another gifts of healing by that one Spirit,10 to another miraculous powers, to another prophecy, to another distinguishing between spirits, to another speaking in different kinds of tongues, and to still another the interpretation of tongues.11 All these are the work of one and the same Spirit, and he distributes them to each one, just as he determines.

Memory Verse 1 Corinthians 12:4 CEB
[4]There are different spiritual gifts but the same Spirit;

Rhyme Time
What the Lord has done
Compares to no one

Insight:

There are many more gifts also found in the Old Testament and many references in New Testament and how God used them through many people, from kings to paupers. The gifts are the "machinery" that God uses in the life of the believer to do His will.

The Apostle writes to young Timothy in 2 Timothy 1:6-7 NKJV [6] Therefore I remind you to stir up the gift of God which is in you through the laying on of my hands. [7] For God has not given us a spirit of fear, but of power and of love and of a sound mind. We have been given a gift from God!

This is our offensive weapon in the Word of God. All the others are protective in nature.

This Spiritual armor is to remain on you!

1 Peter 4:10 NIV
each of you should use whatever gift you have received to serve others, as faithful stewards of God's grace in its various forms.

Let us continue to **H.O.P.E.** in God
1. **Humble, Obey, Pray, Everyday**
2. Be always aware of the Armor of God upon you.
3. As you live and move and have your being let the fruit of the Spirit reflect your character at all times.
4. A man's gift makes room for him and brings him before the great. Proverbs 18:16 ESV

It says in Ephesians 3:20-21 NKJV
Now to Him who is able to do exceedingly abundantly above all that we ask or think, according to the power that works in us,21 to Him be glory in the church by Christ Jesus to all generations, forever and ever. Amen.

That power at work in us is the HOLY SPIRIT.
Receive His Word.
Believe His Word.
Live His Word. God sends revival. Let God revive you Now!

Your Thoughts:

GOD IS LOVE

A. GOD IS LOVE

Those who do not love do not know God because God is love. 1 John 4:8 NLV

While we were still sinners, God Loved us. Romans 5:8 NLV

The two greatest commandments   Matthew 22:36-40 NKJV

vs 36 "Teacher, which is the GREAT COMMANDMENT in the law"?

vs 37 Jesus then said to them, "you shall love the Lord your God with all your heart, with ail your soul and with all your mind." Also in Deuteronomy 6:5 and Leviticus 19:18

vs 38 "This is the FIRST and great commandment."

vs 39 and the SECOND is like it, "you shall love your neighbor as yourself"

Vs 40 On these TWO commandments hang all the law and the prophets".

From this we understand that we are too:
1. Love God totally, completely.
2. Love one another unconditionally.
3. God's love for one another covers a multitude of sins.1 Peter 4:8

So, if the commandments of God are to love Him and all people, should we not live in God's love?

It is not a choice for a follower of Christ. It is clear in 1John 4: 7-9 NIV

Vs 7 Dear friends, let us love one another, for love comes from God. Everyone who loves has been born of God and knows God. Vs 8 Whoever does not love does not know God, because God is love. Vs 9 This is how God showed his love among us, He sent his one and only Son into the world that we might live through him.

B. CHARACTERISTIC OR ATTITUDES OF GOD'S LOVE.

1 Corinthians 13:1-8 NIV

verses 1-3 say that God's love is most important over all others things.

Vs4	Love is:	patient
		kind
vs4	Love is NOT:	envious
		boastful
		prideful
vs5	Love is NOT:	rude
		self-centered

		provoked
		thinking evil thoughts
vs6	Love is NOT:	happy with sin
	love	rejoices in the truth
vs7	love	bears all things
		believes all things
		hopes all things
		endures all things
vs8		love never fails

Hatred stirs up strife, But love covers all sins. Proverbs 10:12 NKJV

C. GOD'S LOVE IS HEALTHY

A happy heart is good medicine *and* a joyful mind causes healing,
But a broken spirit dries up the bones. Proverbs 17:22 AMP. Also in Isaiah 53:5, James 5:16, Malachi 4:2, 3 John 2.
The American Medical Association says that people who have a good attitude heal faster than those who have much stress in their lives.

D. GOD'S LOVE GIVES POWER TO LOVE YOUR ENEMIES.

But I say, love your enemies! Pray for those who persecute you! Matthew 5:44 NLT
Read also Matthew 5 verses 45 through 48 and Romans 12:14.

E. GOD'S LOVE CASTS OUT ALL FEAR.

No fear in love 1 John 4:18-21.

Summarize:
A. GOD IS LOVE
B. GOD'S CHARACTERISTICS OF LOVE
C. GOD'S LOVE IS HEALTHY
D. GOD'S LOVE HAS POWER
E. GOD'S LOVE IS FEARLESS.

Note: The word "love" appears 551 times in the New International Version.
The Bible is the Book of God's Love.

Memory Verse 1 John 4:11 NIV
Dear friends, since God so loved us, we also ought to love one another.

Rhyme Time
God's people
Love all people

Insight:

A hit song in 1965 was ""What the World Needs Now Is Love ". with lyrics by Hal David and music by Burt Bacharach.

Close but not close enough. What the World needs now is God's love! Certainly, among believers and followers in Christ, we should be the witness of Christ's unconditional love to the world.

Your Thoughts:

P.R.A.Y.

The Lord's Prayer. Matthew 6:9-13

"The earnest (heartfelt, continued) prayer of a righteous man makes tremendous power available {dynamic in its working}." James 5:16b AMP

Jesus must become more important, while I become less important John 3:30.CEV. In essence, we want to prepare to enter into a dialogue with God and we must enter with our hearts and spirits guiltless and blameless. This comes through repentance and accepting His forgiveness for our sins.

P- prepare our hearts. Humble, confess, repent, God will forgive your sins. 1 John 1:8-10

> "If My people who are called by My name, will humble themselves and pray, and seek my face and turn from their wicked ways, then will I hear from heaven and will forgive their sin and will heal their land." 2 Chronicles. 7:14 NIV

R-revere His name.

> Fear & worship God. Psalms.22:23; 2:11; 25:14; 112:1;115:15;
>
> Also in Proverbs 2:1-5 NCV
>
> Fear the LORD, you chosen people of his, for those who fear him lack nothing.
>
> Psalms 34:9 MEV
> Fear here means worship, awe reverence, to marvel. This is holy fear (awe) because of who He is. These benefits in Proverbs 2 are yours If you do these: v1, Receive His word, treasure His commands, v2 listen to wisdom and apply your heart to understanding. v3, Yes, cry out for wisdom and beg for understanding, v4, Search for it as for silver, hunt for it like hidden treasure. Then read the rest of Psalm 2.

A-acknowledge our dependence on Him.

> Make Him Lord and Savior John.13:13
> Never seen the righteous forsaken Psalms 37:25
> Can do nothing without Him John 15:5
> His presence is always with you Deuteronomy 31:6.
> We have the mind of Christ 1 Corinthians 2:16.

Y-yield ourselves in obedience to His will.

Not everyone who says to Me 'Lord, Lord' will enter the kingdom of heaven but only he who does the will of my Father who is in heaven." Matthew 7:21 NIV.

We read also in Also James 4:7, Hebrews 12:9 Matthew 26:42

Give in! Let God have right of way with you, let His way and His thoughts be yours.

Here it is simply stated:

Prepare, Revere, Acknowledge, Yield

During prayer we can receive:

1. Decision making
2. Direction
3. Guidance
4. Insight
5. Prophecy (yours & others)
6. Rest for spirit and soul
7. Revelation
8. Visions
9. Miracles
10. Healings
11. Happiness
12. Forgiveness
13. Wisdom
14. Deliverance
15. Understanding
16. Calling
17. Knowledge

TO NAME SOME!!

Remember John 4:23 ...the true worshipper will worshiper the Father in spirit and truth...

Memory Verse 1 Thessalonians 5:17 LEB
Pray constantly

Rhyme Time
Pray to keep in touch
His blessings are so much

Insight:

There are so many ways to pray to God. I like the story of the lineman on top of a telephone pole overhearing three people below talking about the best position to pray in. One said while sitting he felt closest to God, another said standing was his best position, the third said he found lying down was best position for him to pray. At that time the lineman hollered below and said "I couldn't help but overhear your discussion about the best position you believe for prayer, the best way I've found to pray is, while I was hanging upside down by one leg on top of a telephone pole" Obviously, what really is important is the attitude not position for prayer. Of course our heart position must be right

Your Thoughts:

THE SERMON ON THE MOUNT

Matthew 5:1-12 Amplified Version

The Latin word for Beatitudes is Beatus and means Happy or Blessed.
Synonyms; joy · divine rapture · saintliness · sainthood. blessedness · benediction · grace · bliss · ecstasy · exaltation · supreme happiness · heavenly

Matthew 5:1-12 AMP
When Jesus saw the crowds, He went up on the mountain; and when He was seated, His [a] disciples came to Him. [2] Then He *began* to teach them, saying,

[3] "Blessed [spiritually prosperous, happy, to be admired] are the poor in spirit [those devoid of spiritual arrogance, those who regard themselves as insignificant], for theirs is the kingdom of heaven [both now and forever].

[4] "Blessed [forgiven, refreshed by God's grace] are those who mourn [over their sins and repent], for they will be comforted [when the burden of sin is lifted].

[5] "Blessed [inwardly peaceful, spiritually secure, worthy of respect] are the [b]gentle [the kind-hearted, the sweet-spirited, the self-controlled], for they will inherit the earth.

[6] "Blessed [joyful, nourished by God's goodness] are those who hunger and thirst for righteousness [those who actively seek right standing with God], for they will be [completely] satisfied.

[7] "Blessed [content, sheltered by God's promises] are the merciful, for they will receive mercy.

[8] "Blessed [anticipating God's presence, spiritually mature] are the pure in heart [those with integrity, moral courage, and godly character.]

[9] "Blessed [spiritually calm with life-joy in God's favor] are the makers *and* maintainers of peace, for they will [express His character and] be called the sons of God.

[10] "Blessed [comforted by inner peace and God's love] are those who are persecuted for doing that which is morally right, for theirs is the kingdom of heaven [both now and forever].

[11] "Blessed [morally courageous and spiritually alive with life-joy in God's goodness] are you when *people* insult you and persecute you, and falsely say all kinds of evil things against you because of [your association with] Me.

[12] Be glad and exceedingly joyful, for your reward in heaven is great [absolutely inexhaustible]; for in this same way they persecuted the prophets who were before you.

Memory Verse Matthew 5:3 NKJV
"Blessed *are* the poor in spirit,
For theirs is the kingdom of heaven.

Rhyme Time
When God is your rest
You will be blessed

Insight:

The beatitudes, statements of characteristics and blessing, are part of the Sermon on the Mount that Jesus spoke and is recorded in Matthew 5:1-12

Each beatitude looks at different circumstances of life and how all Christians are blessed through their faith.

Through these beatitudes, Jesus teaches of virtues and values in life that will result in blessings and rewards.

The scriptures will encourage you and give you hope as you face each day knowing that you are called blessed! No matter your age, job, or family role, or ethnic group if you apply the beatitudes in your life you will experience one fulfilled in Christ!

Your Thoughts:

ARMOR OF GOD

EPHESIANS 6:10-18 NLT

Vs 10   A final word: Be strong in the Lord and in his mighty power.
         "The joy of the Lord is my strength
         Have joy! A fruit of the Spirit,
         Empowered by the Holy Spirit.
         And in the power of His might

         Power = ability to act or produce an affect.
         Almighty God in His might He is Omnipotent
         Power in Holy Spirit Ephesians 3:20
         Power that works in us"

Vs 11   Put on all of God's armor so that you will be able to stand firm against all
         Strategies of the devil.

         Put on, Suit up Dress up, put on your spiritual battle uniform
         Stand in grace against the threats of the devil.
         God give us favor, grace, mercy and blessings.
         Combat armor is what military and police use in the natural defense against enemies.
         Our enemy can come to our homes through radio, TV, video, magazines, internet,
         etc... Need to keep armor on 24/7/365

Vs 12   For we[a] are not fighting against flesh-and-blood enemies, but against evil rulers
         and authorities of the unseen world, against mighty powers in this dark world, and
         against evil spirits in the heavenly places.

         Not fighting with man, people, relatives, friends, enemies.
         But against spiritual groups of wickedness in the Heavenly places.
         Not seen by human eye. Can't grab it.

Vs 13   Therefore, put on every piece of God's armor so you will be able to resist the enemy
         in the time of evil. Then after the battle you will still be standing firm.

         Greater is He in you than he who is in the World. 1John 4:4 So, keep your armor on!
         So we can stay standing in evil (bad) days
         Due to sadness, depression, trials, tribulations, losses, sickness, struggles, emotional
         upheavals, divorce temptations etc...

Vs 14 Stand your ground, putting on the belt of truth and the body armor of God's righteousness

> ***Stand***
> > ***Tough***
> > > ***Against***
> > > > ***Numerous***
> > > > > ***Demons/devils.***

Jesus is the Truth John 14:6, and John 8:32.

Put on the breast plate of righteousness, integrity, and of strong moral conduct. To be righteous is to be in right standing with God. He is our righteousness. We are righteous because of accepting Jesus Christ as Lord and Savior. Righteousness is the state of moral perfection required by God to enter Heaven. Remember Galatians 5:19-21. Works of the flesh.

Vs 15 For shoes, put on the peace that comes from the Good News so that you will be fully prepared.

Protect your feet Put on good footwear, firm footed, stability, be ready. Put on peace (Prince of Peace is Christ) so that you will be fully prepared to share the Good News (Gospel) with sure footing.

Vs 16 In addition to all of these, hold up the shield of faith to stop the fiery arrows of the devil.

Lift up over all the armor, the shield of saving faith, which will stop all the weapons of the devil against you.

Vs 17 Put on salvation as your helmet, and take the sword of the Spirit, which is the word of God.

Put on your helmet of salvation. The army now has bullet proof helmets!
Know that you are saved by Christ alone and no other gospel. And Sword of Spirit which is the Word of God.

Vs 18 Pray in the Spirit at all times and on every occasion. Stay alert and be persistent in your prayers for all believers everywhere.[

Stay alert! Watch out for your great enemy, the devil. He prowls around like a roaring lion, looking for someone to devour. 1 Peter 58 NLT

Memory Verse Jeremiah 33:3 NKJV
'Call to me and I will answer you, and show you
Great and mighty things, which you do not know'

Rhyme Time
The armor of God protects us from evil
So we don't become sinful

Insight:

Having the proper equipment in doing your job, whatever it may be, e.g. Doctor, lawyer, fireman etc., is essential in being effective in doing a great job. How much more are believers to be spiritually equipped for when the enemy of our soul (devil & demons) comes around? This is how we overcome the enemy and have victory in Christ. What a witness to all who see our good works through faith in Christ.

Your Thoughts:

The Whole Armor of God
Ephesians 6:10-18

Suffer hardship with me as a good soldier of Christ Jesus. No soldier in active service entangles himself in the affairs of everyday life, so that he may please the one who has enlisted him as a soldier, and if anyone competes as an athlete, he does not win the prize unless he competes according to the rules.
2 Timothy 2:3-5

The Helmet of Salvation
Verse-17

The Breastplate of Righteousness
Verse-14
1 Corinthians 1:30

The Shield of Faith
Verse-16
Hebrews 11

The Belt of Truth
Verse-14
John 8:31-32 John 14:6

The Sword of The Spirit
Verse-17
Hebrews 4:12-13

Feet Shod with The Gospel
Verse-15
Romans 10:15

10 Finally, be strong in the Lord, and in the strength of his might.

11 Put on the whole armor of God, that ye may be able to stand against the wiles of the devil.

12 For our wrestling is not against flesh and blood, but against the principalities, against the powers, against the world-rulers of this darkness, against the spiritual hosts of wickedness in the heavenly places.

13 Wherefore take up the whole armor of God, that ye may be able to withstand in the evil day, and, having done all, to stand.

14 Stand therefore, having girded your loins with truth, and having put on the breastplate of righteousness,

15 and having shod your feet with the preparation of the gospel of peace;

16 withal taking up the shield of faith, wherewith ye shall be able to quench all the fiery darts of the evil one.

17 And take the helmet of salvation, and the sword of the Spirit, which is the word of God:

18 with all prayer and supplication praying at all seasons in the Spirit, and watching thereunto in all perseverance and supplication for all the saints,

YOUR LIFE IS YOUR TESTIMONY

(Witness for Christ)

"But you shall receive power when the Holy Spirit has come upon you; and you shall be witnesses to Me in Jerusalem, and in all Judea and Samaria, and to the end of the earth."
Acts 1:8 NKJV

Jesus spent 3 years with the apostles.
New Testament documents the relationship through His Son Jesus Christ as our Savior, through teachings, sharing and showing through demonstration of signs, wonders, healing, deliverance and miracles.

The Old Testament tells how people related to God and how God wanted to relate to them.
See Section 1 page 9 for more names of God.
These are some of the Names defining God's nature and character;
Jehovah Shammah (the Lord is there). Abraham offering Isaac as sacrifice.
Jehovah Jireh the Lord provides;
Jehovah Raphe the Lord our healer;
Jehovah Shalom Lord of peace,
Jehovah Eli the Lord my God;
Jehovah Moshiekh the Lord our Savior.

Today, the Word has not changed. Hebrews 13:8 NLT Jesus Christ *is* the same yesterday, today, and forever.

To live our life in God we must pursue in three areas;

1. Be a God seeker.
    Find God, Jeremiah. 29:13, seek Him find Him = blessings, Matthew 6:33

    Need His ever present in us. You are the temple of Holy Spirit who takes up residence in you.

    These scriptures tell us how to seek Him;
    1 Chronicles 28:9 charge to Solomon.
    2 Chronicles 7:14 Humble yourself, pray, seek God and turn from sinful ways.
    Jeremiah 33:3 call on Him
    Proverbs 8:17 Loves those who seek Him
    Proverbs 8:35 Finds Him will receive favor

2. Knowing Christ personally.
    Fellowship with Christ
    God is faithful, who has called you into fellowship with his Son, Jesus Christ our Lord.
    1 Corinthians 1:9 ESV
    Free in Christ (saved) John 8:32,33,36
    Feed on Christ "Just as the living Father sent Me, and I live because of the Father, so he
    one who feeds on Me will live because of Me." John 6:57 NKJV

3. Serve Christ.
    If anyone serves Me, let him follow Me; and where I am, there My servant will be also.
    If anyone serves Me, him *My* Father will honor. John 12:26 NKJV

    Follow Christ and he said to all, "If anyone would come after me, he must deny himself,
    take up his cross and follow me." Luke 9:23 ESV

    Remain in Christ. As the Father loved Me, I also have loved you; abide in My love. John
    15:9 ESV

    Obey Christ. If you love Me, keep My commandments. John 14:15 NIV
    Be filled with the Holy Spirit. Ephesians 5:18

    Seek God
    Know Christ personally
    Imitate Christ in your life.

    AND you will bring glory to God (highest form of worship)!become a victor not a victim.
    Overcome the world by the blood of Christ and word of testimony. Revelation 12:11

Memory verse Matthew 10:18 NIV
On my account you will be brought before governors and kings
as witnesses to them and to the Gentiles.

Rhyme time
You may have little or much money
But what is your testimony

Insight:

People are watching you without your knowledge. What will they observe in you and your
life style? Will they realize that you are a person seeking God in all you do? Someone who

symbolizes (say and do all the right things) a belief in Christ but has no substance (Does not live their life in God's love.

A hearer of the Word only and not a doer. James 1:22 ESV.

Your thoughts:

DISCIPLINE YOUR LIFE

John 8:31 NKJV If you abide in My word, you are My disciples indeed.

Proverbs 13:24 Disciplining you child means you love him

Also see Proverbs 29:17

Discipline is systematic instruction intended to train a person, sometimes literally called a disciple, in craft or trade or other activity, or to follow a particular code of conduct or order.

1. Learn His Word 2 Timothy 2:15 NKJV
    Be diligent to present yourself approved to God, a worker who does not need to be ashamed, rightly dividing the word of truth.

    With;
    Romans 12:2 CEV Don't be like the people of this world, but let God change the way you think. Then you will know how to do everything that is good and pleasing to him.

    Learn by reading the Bible
    Learn by studying the Bible
    Learn by memorizing scripture
    Learn in study groups
    Learn by studying Bible characters from Old and New Testaments
    Learn by praying, listening, fasting, waiting on the Lord
    Learn by reading devotionals like the Daily Bread
    Learn through writings, hearing the Word (sermons, teachings)
    Use different Bible versions for better comprehension
    Learn origin of words and their meanings (Reference for example, Strong's Exhaustive Concordance)

2. Live His Word John 15:1-7 NKJV
    Stay connected to the TRUE Vine
    1 "I am the true vine, and My Father is the vinedresser. 2 Every branch in Me that does not bear fruit He takes away;[a] and every branch that bears fruit He prunes, that it may bear more fruit. 3 You are already clean because of the word which I have spoken to you.4 Abide in Me, and I in you. As the branch cannot bear fruit of itself, unless it abides in the vine, neither can you, unless you abide in Me. 5 I am the vine, you are the branches. He who abides in Me, and I in him, bears much fruit; for without Me you can do nothing. 6 If anyone does not abide in Me, he is cast out as a branch and is withered; and they gather them and throw them into the fire, and they are burned.7 If you abide in Me, and My words abide in you, you will ask what you desire, and it shall be done for you."

John1:14 The Word is Christ
Live in whole counsel (will) of God Acts 20:27
Apply spiritual principles in your daily living

For example:
Fruit of the Spirit, Galatians 5:22,23
Gifts of the Spirit,! Corinthians 12:1-11
Beatitudes in Matthew 5:1-12 (Sermon on the Mount)
Put on the Armor of God. Ephesians 6:11-18
Pray without ceasing 1 Thessalonians 5:17. Be always ready to pray!
Listen and know God is real Psalm 46:10
Meditate on His Word.

3. Love His Word John 14:21 TLB
The one who obeys me is the one who loves me; and because he loves me, my Father will love him; and I will too, and I will reveal myself to him."

Love the Lord and one another Matthew 22:37-40 NKJV
[37] Jesus said to him," You shall love the LORD your God with all your heart, with all your soul, and with all your mind.' [38] This is the first and great commandment. [39] And the second is like it: 'You shall love your neighbor as yourself.' [40] On these two commandments hang all the Law and the Prophets."

Become intimate with His Word, even as you know and memorize the alphabet. Cherish it, know it, uphold it, defend it.

Christ is the Word. Grow a deep relationship with Christ where you began and continue until His Word becomes part of you, you find answer in your life in His Word. Proverbs are full of His wisdom.

Memory verse Proverbs 12:1 ESV
Whoever loves discipline loves knowledge,
but whoever hates correction is stupid

Rhyme Time
Learn, live, and love Him faithfully
You will be with Him eternally

Insight:

We have been given the spirit of discipline. 2 Timothy 1:7. When we realize that all we need to live a godly life is written in God's Word, then we will receive His discipline in our life

Your thoughts:

REGENERATION AND SPIRITUAL REBIRTH

John 3:3 MEV "Jesus answered and said to him, "Most assuredly, I say to you, unless one is born again, he cannot see the kingdom of God.""

Scriptures regarding new birth:

1. Regeneration is a process:
   A. Eternal life in God.
      Imparted to believer's heart (Impart= to give or reveal)
   B. Becomes a child of God. John 1:12
   C. A new person in Christ. 2 Corinthians 5:17
   D. Do not conform to this world. Romans 12:2
   E. Created to be like God in true righteousness & holiness. Ephesians 4:24

2. Regeneration is Necessary:
   A. Because apart from Christ no one can obey or please God. Romans 8:7-8
   B. Without Christ you can do nothing. John 15:5

3. Regeneration is Repentance:
   A. You must repent of sin, turn to God.
      (Repent = turning from wrongdoing) Matthew 3:2
   B. believe in Jesus Christ as Lord and Savior. Philippians 2:11

4. Regeneration is Sustained by:
   A. Transition from old life to new life (new creation) 2 Corinthians 5:17
      1. Set free from power of sin Romans 6:22
      2. Receive spiritual desire to obey God and Holy Spirit. Romans 8:13-14
      3. Live a righteous life. 1 John 2:29
      4. Love other believers 1 John 4::7-8
      5. Avoid a life of sin 1 John 3:9; 5:18
      6. Do not love the world, Romans 12:2, 1 John 2:15

Memory Verse John 3:3 NKJV
Jesus answered and said to him, "Most assuredly, I say to you, unless one is born again, he cannot see the kingdom of God."

Rhyme Time:
Natural born gives life
Born again gives eternal life

Insight:

As your natural birth is a miracle from God, you now can receive a spiritual birth in Christ. This is a free gift from God. Considering that the benefits are eternal life, what a deal NOT to pass up.

Your thoughts:

T.H.A.W.

Talk. Hear. Answer. Work.
Hebrews 3:8-10 NIV

1. TALK. Pray for, call upon, intercede, petition. Ephesians 6:18, James 5:16
   Talk to the Father in Jesus name. He is God Almighty, Prince of peace, Provider, Lord of lords, God of gods, King of kings, Savior of your soul, Master of your life.

2. HEAR. Listen, be still, be aware, receive, be alert, wait Psalms 37:7; Romans 10:17
   Heard the Holy Spirit will teach you all things. John 14:26.
   God can speak in a still small voice. 1 Kings 19:12

3. ANSWER. Receive Jeremiah 29:12; 33:3
   Answer will come through prayer, Word, revelation, other people, word of wisdom, word of knowledge, tongues and interpretation, prophecy. 1 Corinthians 12, also through dreams, visions, counsel, signs and wonders

4. WORK. Do it, in obedience, follow through, act upon it, work it out! James 1:22.
   Work it out in faith, not on your own understanding. Proverb 3:5-8
   * Take a step of faith.
   * Keep your main thought on the main thought.
   * Timing is everything, don't delay and miss the way!
   * And do the work of the Father. Luke 2:49

   Promises of God found in John 15:7 and 2 Corinthians 1:20

Memory Verse Jeremiah 33:3 NIV
'Call to me and I will answer you
and tell you great and unsearchable things you do not know.'

Rhyme Time
God will not contend with man forever
Begin now to receive His favor

Insight:

A term more used some time ago, "chill out". My teens would use it often. In New England, many people wait for the Spring thaw to come. Some wait all winter for it to bring a change in the weather. Too many believers live in an anticipation of God "thawing" things for us. Whether it be our relationship with Him or others. You may have heard the term "frozen chosen" jokingly referring to believers in the cold Northern states. Yet some may apply it to their relationship to God. It is time to "thaw" out or "chill out" and enter into the warmth of the Lord's love. Don't let your heart be hardened, let the love of God thaw you out!

Your Thoughts:

GOD IS IN THE DETAILS

Let's look at 5 areas where God's detail is extremely important.

1. Anointing Oil: Exodus 30:22-32 NLT
    [22] Then the LORD said to Moses, [23] "Collect choice spices—12 1/2 pounds of pure myrrh, 6 1/4 pounds of fragrant cinnamon, 6 1/4 pounds of fragrant calamus,[a] [24] and 12 1/2 pounds of cassia[b]—as measured by the weight of the sanctuary shekel. Also get one gallon of olive oil.[c] [25] Like a skilled incense maker, blend these ingredients to make a holy anointing oil.
    Read verses 26-31

    [32] It must never be used to anoint anyone else, and you must never make any blend like it for yourselves. It is holy, and you must treat it as holy.

    God is in the detail on exact quantity and mixture and on how to blend the oil.

2. The incense perfume Exodus 30:34-38 NLT
    [34] Then the LORD said to Moses, "Gather fragrant spices—resin droplets, mollusk shell, and galbanum—and mix these fragrant spices with pure frankincense, weighed out in equal amounts. [35] Using the usual techniques of the incense maker, blend the spices together and sprinkle them with salt to produce a pure and holy incense. [38] Anyone who makes incense like this for personal use will be cut off from the community."

    Again, God is in the detail.

3. The temple Solomon built. Found in 1 Kings 5.
    Support from King Hiram by suppling all the lumber needed. King Solomon hired thousands of men throughout Israel to work on the Temple with timber and quarried stone. Material and manpower provided.

    1 Kings 6:2-7 (NLT)
    [2] The Temple that King Solomon built for the LORD was 90 feet long, 30 feet wide, and 45 feet high.[a] [3] The entry room at the front of the Temple was 30 feet[b] wide, running across the entire width of the Temple. It projected outward 15 feet[c] from the front of the Temple.

    [5] He built a complex of rooms against the outer walls of the Temple, all the way around the sides and rear of the building. [6] The complex was three stories high, the bottom floor being 7 1/2 feet wide, the second floor 9 feet wide, and the top floor 10 1/2 feet wide.[a] The rooms were connected to the walls of the Temple by beams resting on ledges built out from the wall. So the beams were not inserted into the walls themselves.

Verse 7 The stones used in the construction of the Temple were finished at the quarry, so there was no sound of hammer, ax, or any other iron tool at the building site.

God gives detailed dimensions to Solomon on the design of the Temple.

Verse 38 It took 7 years to complete. Seven is God's number of perfection, completion.

Other examples of God in the detail;
The detail God commanded for the Ark that Noah built. Genesis 6:14-16
The detail God gave Moses to build the Ark of the Covenant. Exodus 37:1-9

4. God builds Christlike character in His people. Galatians 5:22-23 NLT
   [22] But the Holy Spirit produces this kind of fruit in our lives: love, joy, peace, patience, kindness, goodness, faithfulness, [23] gentleness, and self-control. There is no law against these things!

God gives us His character traits!

5. God gives us protection. Ephesians 6:10-11 NIV
   [10] A final word: Be strong in the Lord and in his mighty power. [11] Put on all of God's armor so that you will be able to stand firm against all strategies of the devil.

God details what we are to use against the enemy!.

Memory Verse Matthew 5:18 NLT
I tell you the truth, until heaven and earth disappear, not even the smallest detail of God's law will disappear until its purpose is achieved.

Rhyme Time
If you don't follow God's detail
You may derail

Insight:

Detail is a part of a whole. To be complete in Christ requires all the details in our life be in place. Try working using the wrong tool or speaking the wrong words! When you seek God in prayer make sure you have taken care of any detail, sin, attitude, unforgiveness or any issues that detract you from entering into His presence.

Your thoughts:

RELIGION OR RELATIONSHIP

Don't let your religion interfere with your relationship with God!

Deuteronomy 4:29 NIV "But if from there you seek the Lord your God, you will find Him if you look for Him with all your heart and with all your soul."
Religion is defined as (short version) Man's attempt to find God.

According to the Holy Bible. The Word of God, if your religious conduct (attempting to find God) is merely in our METHOD, PROGRAMS, DOCTRINES, DOGMAS, CEREMONIES, RITUALS, SERVICE, WORSHIP AND DEVOTIONS without Christ as the center, there is no life. It is a religion with NO Holy Spirit power! Unless Jesus Christ is the focus of our religion, we will fall short and become idolaters.

TRUE RELIGION:
James 1:26-27 NIV "If anyone considers himself religious and yet does not keep a tight rein on his tongue, he deceives himself and his religion is worthless. Religion that God our Father accepts as pure and faultless is this; to look after orphans and widows in their distress and keep oneself from being polluted by the world."

The Apostle Paul's life as an example.
Paul before King Agrippa Acts 26:5 NIV "They have known me for a long time and can testify, if they are willing, that I conformed to the strictest sect of our religion, living as a Pharisee."

Acts 26:9-10 NIV On "I too was convinced that I ought to do all that was possible to oppose the name of Jesus of Nazareth. And that is just what I did in Jerusalem. On the authority of the chief priests I put many of the saints in prison, and when they were put to death, I cast my vote against them."

Saul was a religious man, but without a proper Relationship with God through Jesus Christ. Prior to Paul's conversion on the road to Damascus, God changed Paul's name from Saul to Paul

We read in Acts 26:12-16 "On one of these journeys I was going to Damascus with the authority and commission of the chief priests. About noon, I saw a light from heaven brighter than the sun, blazing around me and my companions. We all fell to the ground, and I heard a voice saying to me in Aramaic, "Saul, Saul, why do you persecute me? It is hard for you to kick against the goads" Then I asked "Who are you Lord?" I am Jesus, whom you are persecuting, the Lord replied. "Now get up and stand on your feet. I have appeared to you to appoint you as a servant and as a witness of what you have seen of me and what I will show you".

As we talk about relationship: Paul personally experienced Christ and developed a relationship with Him.

We experience Christ and develop a relationship beginning at our conversion (the new birth) Born again. (John Chapter 3).

This relationship is God's plan through Jesus Christ to redeem and save man from eternal damnation (Hell).

Jesus prayed for us.

John 17:20-23, 26 NKJV

20 "I do not pray for these alone, but also for those who will believe in Me through their word; 21 that they all may be one, as You, Father, *are in* Me, and I in You; that they also may be one in Us, that the world may believe that You sent Me. 22 And the glory which You gave Me I have given them, that they may be one just as We are one: 23 I in them, and You in Me; that they may be made perfect in one, and that the world may know that You have sent Me, and have loved them as You have loved Me.

Verse 26, And I have declared to them Your name, and will declare *it,* that the love with which You loved Me may be in them, and I in them."

Memory Verse Joshua 24:15b KJV
But as for me an my house, we will serve the Lord

Rhyme Time
You can worship man, money or brass
Or only Christ will last

Insight:

Jesus desires that we have fellowship, intimacy and oneness with Him, God the Father and The Holy Spirit. Don't let your religion interfere with your relationship with God. Whatever we are doing in life, whether in church, work or home we must sustain and build a stronger relationship in Christ.

Your Thoughts:

GOD'S PURPOSE FOR YOU

God's power works through you when these conditions are in place in your life.

A. Be Holy 1 Peter 1:15,16 NIV
But just as he who called you is holy, so be holy in all you do; [16] for it is written: "Be holy, because I am holy."[a]

God desires His people to be have clean hands and a pure heart. Psalm 24:1-7,
Have a good reputation. 1 Timothy 3-7,
Approved by God and man. 2 Timothy 2:14-22
Vessel for honor, prepared to do good works. 2 Timothy 2:21

Root word for Holy
The Hebrew word for holy is "qodesh" and means "apartness, set-apartness, separateness, sacredness" and I would add that it should also be "otherness, transcendent and totally other" because God is totally above His creation and His creatures, including us. Holy has the idea of heaviness or weight of glory. In the New Testament, the word for holy is "hagios" and means set apart, reverend, sacred, and worthy of veneration." This word applies to God because God Himself is totally separate, sacred, transcendent, reverend, and set apart from every created thing. Since God is spirit this is why the third person of the Trinity is called the Holy Spirit. He too is fully God and all three persons of the Trinity are holy and have the weight of glory abounding in them.

Holy, Holy, Holy
God has many attributes characteristics), God is merciful, patient, long suffering, and abounding in love, there is an attribute of God that is mentioned three times and is His predominant attribute. He is not just Holy, but He is Holy, Holy, Holy. In Jewish liturgy, when something is incredibly important, it is mentioned twice. Jesus does this when He says something twice like "verily, verily" but this also signifies great intimacy when He repeats someone's name twice like Moses, Moses; Abraham, Abraham; Saul, Saul...but when something is mentioned three times in a row, it is off the charts in importance, this is why all the attributes of God He is holy, holy, holy. That is the greatest emphasis that can be put on anything or anyone in Scripture and this is telling us that this is the most important thing about God. God is holy, holy, holy. This is the only attribute of God that is mentioned in the Scriptures three times!

B. Believing His Word
Hebrews 4:12 NIV For the word of God is alive and active. Sharper than any double-edged sword, it penetrates even to dividing soul and spirit, joints and marrow; it judges the thoughts and attitudes of the heart.

Believe His word. Believe for the actual something that the Spirit is telling you, It will always agree with his Word. When we know his word, we know what it says and let the Spirit bring his word to life in you, let Him demonstrate what He will do through you. He gives different spiritual gifts to each one of us. 1 Corinthians Chapters 12 and 14. Also found in Romans 12. Matthew 21:22, John 20:31, 1 Peter 1:8

C. Obey/Action

Matthew 19:17 ESV "Why do you ask me about what is good?" Jesus replied. "There is only One who is good. If you want to enter life, keep the commandments."

Luke 2:49 And He said to them, How is it that you had to look for Me? Did you not see *and* know that it is necessary [as a duty] for Me [a]to be in My Father's house *and* [occupied] about My Father's business? (AMPC)

> Obey Him in action/work. Put your faith in the work he is leading you to do. (faith without works is dead).
> And you are witnesses to these things, "and so is the Holy Spirit, whom God has given to those who obey him."
> Acts 5:32 ESV

"In the year that King Uzziah died I saw the Lord sitting upon a throne, high and lifted up; and the train of his robe filled the temple. Above him stood the seraphim. Each had six wings: with two he covered his face, and with two he covered his feet, and with two he flew. And one called to another and said: "Holy, holy, holy is the Lord of hosts; the whole earth is full of his glory!" And the foundations of the thresholds shook at the voice of him who called, and the house was filled with smoke." Isaiah 6:1-4 ESV

"And the four living creatures, each of them with six wings, are full of eyes all around and within, and day and night they never cease to say, "Holy, holy, holy, is the Lord God Almighty, who was and is and is to come!" Revelation 4:8 ESV

Memory Verse Philippians 1:6 NKJV
Being confident of this very thing, that He who has begun a good
work in you will Complete *it* until the day of Jesus Christ;

Rhyme Time
Be holy, believe and obey
Is God's only way

Insight:

These three areas of your life, 1. Be holy, 2. Believe His word and 3. Obey His calling, will always produce good works in you for His glory.

Since God called us to be holy means we can be holy by the power of His Word and Spirit in us.

Your thoughts:

WONDERFUL WORD OF GOD

Isiah 55:10-11 NLV [10] The rain and snow come down from heaven and do not return there without giving water to the earth. This makes plants grow on the earth, and gives seeds to the planter and bread to the eater. [11] So My Word which goes from My mouth will not return to Me empty. It will do what I want it to do, and will carry out My plan well.

A. The Word is His Story (history of God) contained in the bible.
    Romans 10:14-15 how, then, can they call on the one they have not believed in? And how can they believe in the one of whom they have not heard? And how can they hear without someone preaching to them? 15 And how can anyone preach unless they are sent? As it is written: "How beautiful are the feet of those who bring good news!"

    Matthew 4:4 NLV But Jesus said, "It is written, 'Man is not to live on bread only. Man is to live by every word that God speaks.'"

    God speaking directly to people. Genesis 12:1-2 (Abram).
    God speaks through prophets to address His People. Jerimiah 1,7.
    God gives and speaks through apostles, prophets, pastors, teachers and evangelist. Ephesians 4:11-12

    Jesus is the Word of God. John 1:1,14
    Jesus speaks the Word of God. Mark 1:14,15
    Gospel is the good news.

B. Power of the Word
    Romans 1:16. Gospel (word) is the power of God to save.
    2 Timothy 3:16. NLT All Scripture is inspired by God and is useful to teach us what is true and to make us realize what is wrong in our lives. It corrects us when we are wrong and teaches us to do what is right.

    1 John 2:20 NKJV But you have an anointing from the Holy One, and all of you know the truth.

    Anoint is to be set apart for divine use (Power). Jesus Christ is the Holy One.
    God's power is limitless. He is the Creator of all things visible and invisible. Colossians 1:16

C. Our response to His Word.
    2 Timothy 2:15...correctly handles the Word of Truth....
    James 1:22-25, not only hear but do the word...
    Luke 2:49 MEV [49] He said to them, "How is it that you searched for Me? Did you not know that I must be about My Father's business?" All Scripture is inspired by God and is useful

to teach us what is true and to make us realize what is wrong in our lives. It corrects us when we are wrong and teaches us to do what is right.

Romans 12:2.MEV [2] Do not be conformed to this world, but be transformed by the renewing of your mind, that you may prove what is the good and acceptable and perfect will of God [2] Do not be conformed to this world, but be transformed by the renewing of your mind, that you may prove what is the good and acceptable and perfect will of God.

There are many ways we can hear from God through our prayers, reading, listening to the Holy Spirit, through other people, teaching, preaching, prophecies, insights, word wisdom, word of knowledge to name some.

Being still before the Lord may take an effort on our part but it can be extremely important to hear His wisdom.

Be still and know that I am God. Psalm 46:10 NIV

Jesus said in John 10:27 "My sheep listen to my voice, I know them, and they follow me".

It is Most important to obey that which the Holy Spirit would tell you. As you are led by the Holy Spirit you will be in God's will and His power is resident in you.

Here are some results that we can expect when we respond to God's will and way:
Saved, sanctified, healed, delivered, receive mercy, grace, favor, understanding, instruction.
All the Fruit of the Spirit Galatians 5:22,23
All the Gifts of the Spirit 1 Corinthians Chapter 12
The full Armor of God Ephesians 6:10-17

Memory Verse: 1 John 2:20 NKJV
but you have an anointing from the Holy One
and all of you know the truth

Rhyme Time
When you know God's Word is true
Life will be wonderful for you

Insight:

When we spend time daily with the Lord, He will allow all His power (anointing) to work within us.

Nothing is impossible with God, Matthew 19:25,26 CEV "When the disciples heard this, they were greatly astonished and asked, "Who then can be saved?" "Jesus looked at them and said, "With man this is impossible, but with God all things are possible." Know who you are in Jesus Christ, according to His Word, and begin to receive all He has for you.

Your Thoughts:

DOCTRINE OF CHRIST

(Basic teachings of Christ from the Bible)

A. Commanded.

    Matthew 22:37-40
        1. Love God
        2. Love neighbor
        This fulfills, completes, the Law and Prophets

    John 3:16 God Loved the world—sent His Son
    John 13:34 We are Love one another
    John 14:23 If you really love me—keep my commands
    John 15:17 Commanded—love one another
    1John 4:20 If you hate your brother (other people)—does not love God

B. Do Father's will.

    Luke 2:49 About the Father's business
    Matt 7:21-23 Do will of Father in Heaven
    Matt 6:10 How to pray—Your will be done
    John 6:38 Not my will but the will of Him Who sent Me
    John 6:40 God's will is—believe in His Son, Jesus Christ for eternal life

C. Go Make Disciples.

    Matthew 28:18-20
    Baptize them—public decision
    Teach all I have commanded you
    Commanded to:
        1. Love God
        2. Love Neighbor
        3. Do God's Will
        4. Believe in Christ
        5. Go—do Kingdom work

Memory Verse 1John 4:8 ESV
He who does not love does not know God, for God is love.

Rhyme Time
With correct doctrine
Your faith will be locked in

Insight:

Churches can confuse the Gospel message with their doctrine. For example some churches would tell you;

"Don't smoke, don't drink, don't dance and don't go out with girls who do. Using these guidelines for behavior, as if by doing them you would somehow become more righteous."

Righteousness is only through Jesus Christ!

Not saved by works. Only by God's grace through Jesus Christ. (Ephesians 2:8)

Whenever you find yourself in any

* *Community of believers
* *Fellowship of saints
* *Churches
* *Home cells
* *Bible studies
* *Christian gatherings, seminars, conferences, prayer meeting or any "coming together" as believers in Christ, these fundamental core values and teachings must be present. Doing God's Will out of love

Your Thoughts:

BE

Aware, Alert, Active

1. BE AWARE;
   Of God's Word in you

   Of who you are in Christ

   Believe (faith in Jesus Christ as Savior of your soul and Master of your life), read, study, memorize, obey, speak, share, testify, defend, aware of fruit, and gifts, keep armor of God on

   Be aware of your authority in Christ; Luke 4:18-19

   Be aware of the Holy Spirit within you 1Corinthians 6:19

   Be aware of Jesus anointing you. 1 John 2:20-27.

2. BE ALERT;
   As a watchman; observe, focus on your surroundings and warning sign of danger, be alert to a check in your spirit by the Holy Spirit.

   Know the work of the devil. John 10:10

   Be humble in the presence of God's mighty power, and he will honor you when the time comes, 1 Peter 5:6-9

3. BE ACTIVE;
   As a worker, 2 Timothy 2:15

   In faith doing good deeds. James 2:14

   Do greater things, John 14:12-14

   Jesus gave us the Keys of the Kingdom, Matthew 16:15-19

GOSPEL IN HAND

Your hand has many functions and uses. I want to show you another way God can use your hand as a reminder to bring the Gospel to others. See diagram next page.

1. THUMB, Love God
   Thumbs up for God, is an act, or gesture of ascent, approval Let's use thumbs up as a reminder to love God.

   In Matthew 22:35-36 the Pharisees asked Jesus, Teacher, which is the greatest commandment in the Law? Matthew 22:37 NCV Jesus replied "Love the Lord your God with all your heart and with all your soul and with all your mind. This is the first and greatest commandment".

2. INDEX FINGER, Love people
   Moving side to side gesture means NO, admonish gesture. Pointing it at someone or something brings attention to object. Could be used to summon someone. Or pointing upward could be a gesture of victory, can be used to condemn, find fault, to blame or emphasize a point. Let's use it when we point to someone as a reminder that God loves them and so do we.

   In Matthew 22:39-40 NIV "and the second is like it: Love your neighbor as yourself". All the law and the Prophets hang on these two commandments".

3. MIDDLE finger, Do God's will.
   In an upward position used as obscene or offensive gesture
   Let's use it as a reminder to do God's Will.

   Matthew 7:21-23 CEV Not everyone who calls me their Lord will get into the kingdom of Heaven. Only the ones who obey my Father in heaven will get in. [22] On the day of judgment many will call me their Lord. They will say, "We preached in your name, and in your name, and in your we forced out demons and worked many miracles." [23] But I will tell them, "I will have nothing to do with you! Get out of my sight, you evil people!"

4. RING FINGER Love Jesus
   Let's use it as a reminder to commit your life to Jesus.
   Refers to commitment as in engagement, marriage symbol of covenant

   John 6:40 CEV My Father wants everyone who sees the Son to have faith in him and to have eternal life. Then I will raise them to life on the last day.

5. PINKY Finger Good grip
   Now we have a full grip, let us carry the Gospel everywhere!

Matthew 28:18-20 CEV Jesus came to them and said: I have been given all authority in heaven and on earth! [19] Go to the people of all nations and make them my disciples. Baptize them in the name of the Father, the Son, and the Holy Spirit, [20] and teach them to do everything I have told you. I will be with you always, even until the end of the world.

Your Thoughts:

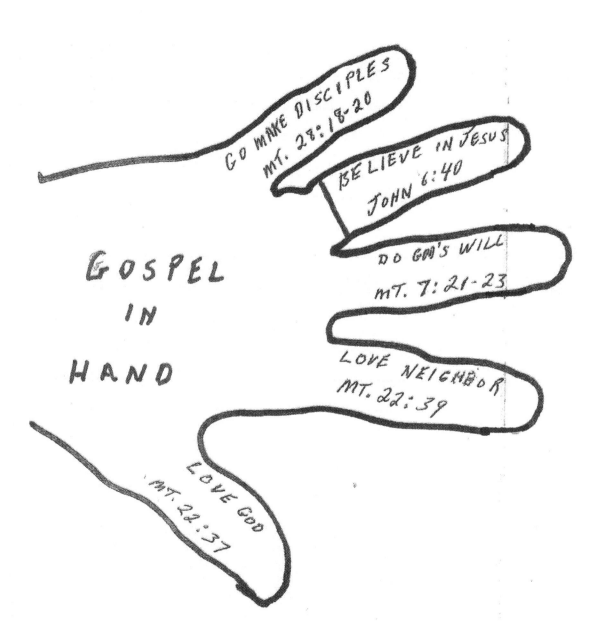

Drawn by R. Couture used by permission

NUMBER YOUR DAYS

Psalm 90:12 -Wisdom NIV
"So teach us to number our days,
That we may gain a heart of wisdom."
Wisdom is comprehensive insight into the ways and purposes of God

3 Types of people's use of time:

1. Living and seeking in the Kingdom of God
    You are using time to seek God and His Will.
    Matthew 6:33 NIV. But seek first his kingdom and his righteousness, and all these things will be given to you as well.

    Seek: implies being continually absorbed in or searching for something. Like a precious possession. That is to seek His Kingdom i.e. God's Will and plan for us.

    Romans 14:17 NIV for the kingdom of God is not eating and drinking, but righteousness and peace and joy in the Holy Spirit.

    Seek His righteousness. Righteous means right standing with God by trusting and obeying His word.

    You are a living testimony of Gods' Grace. You are growing in the Fruit of the Spirit, Galatians 5:22-23 and Gifts of the Spirit 1 Corinthians 12.

    2 Corinthians 4:16 "Therefore we do not lose heart. Even though our outward man is perishing, yet the inward man is being renewed day by day."

2. Religious, any religion (but not committed to Christ)
    You may be doing church attendance, bible studies, memorization, ministry or other worthwhile activities, but transformation in you is not complete.
    You adhere much to the world view and less about Gods' ways.

    You have a form of godliness but denying its power. 2 Timothy 3:5
    Romans 12:2 NIV "and do not be conformed to this world, but be transformed by the renewing of your mind, that you may prove what is that good and acceptable and perfect will of God".

    Acts 3:19 NIV "Repent therefore and be converted, that your sins may be blotted out, so that times of refreshing may come from the presence of the Lord,"

3. Just existing
   You are living and believing in the world view perspective and not in the Biblical word view.

   The Bible contains 66 books written by 40 authors over thousands of years with the main theme of God's love for His creation.

   There are hundreds of prophecies and fulfillment of a coming Savior and Lord Jesus Christ. Prophecies being fulfilled thousands of years after they were proclaimed. How much more evidence would one need?

   I refer you to Josh McDowell's book "Evidence that demands a Verdict". You may also be interested in looking on the Web Peter Stoner's "Mathematical Probability that Jesus is the Christ."

   The scriptures are clear in John 3:16 NIV "For God so loved the world that He gave His only begotten Son, that whoever believes in Him should not perish but have everlasting life. 17 For God did not send His Son into the world to condemn the world, but that the world through Him might be saved.

   Romans 3:23-26 NLV
   23 For all men have sinned and have missed the shining-greatness of God. 24 Anyone can be made right with God by the free gift of His loving-favor. It is Jesus Christ Who bought them with His blood and made them free from their sins. 25 God gave Jesus Christ to the world. Men's sins can be forgiven through the blood of Christ when they put their trust in Him. God gave His Son Jesus Christ to show how right He is. Before this, God did not look on the sins that were done. 26 But now God proves that He is right in saving men from sin. He shows that He is the One Who has no sin. God makes anyone right with Himself who puts his trust in Jesus.

   Romans 5:8 NLV
   But God showed His love to us. While we were still sinners, Christ died for us.

   Romans 10:1-3 NKJV Brethren, my heart's desire and prayer to God for Israel is that they may be saved. 2 For I bear them witness that they have a zeal [or God, but not according^ to knowledge 3 For they being ignorant of God's righteousness,

Memory Verse: Psalm 90:12 NLT
Teach us to realize the brevity of life, so that we may grow in wisdom.

Rhyme Time:
If you let God order your day
You will find the right way

Insight:

Time is common, 24/7 to each of us. What we do with time determines your lifestyle, destiny and your eternity. We must have a proper view of eternity to know the real value of time. So stay the course, run the race, to win the prize at the end (eternal life). Decide whom you will serve, God or Baal (man). Time does not stop, decide now to receive Christ as Savior and Lord, the benefits are eternal.

Your thoughts:

KEEP YOUR FREEDOM

Galatians 5:1-26 (paraphrased

1. Freedom from power of sin. Vs 1
2. Legalism separates us from God Vs 2-4
3. By faith in Christ is righteousness with God. Vs 5-6
4. Pursuing truth "who cut you off?' NOT God but subtly, slowly like yeast in bread. Vs 7-9
5. Truth will prevail whoever leads you astray will be punished. Vs 10
6. Powerless preaching doesn't solve any issues Vs 11
   The truth will be unpopular and followed by persecution.
7. Called to be free. from law, circumcision Vs 12
   Freedom not to sin but to serve.
   The law of God: is to love your neighbor as yourself.
   If you keep hurting and offending each other you will destroy each other. Vs 13-15
8. These verses show the different characteristics of those who live in the flesh, (human nature) or guided by Holy Spirit vs 16-26

   A. There is a struggle between the flesh and the Holy Spirit. vs16-18.
      1. these are acts of flesh(sinful nature):
         sexual unfaithfulness
         not pure
         sexual sins, having no shame or public decency.
         worshiping other gods.
         witchcraft, sorcery
         hatred, extreme dislike (God hates sin)
         quarreling
         jealousy
         anger
         selfishness
         diverse teaching
         faction, division among people
         envy
         drunkenness
         orgies, wild and wasteful parties
         Continuing to do the things will keep you from inheriting the Kingdom of God. vs 19-21

      2. The fruit of the Spirit are produced by the Holy Spirit in you.
         a. love
         b. joy

c. peace
d. patience
e. kindness
f. goodness
g. faithfulness
h. gentleness.
i. self-control

Memory Vs Galatians 5:6 NKJV

For in Christ Jesus neither circumcision nor uncircumcision avails anything,
but faith working through love

Rhyme Time:

The truth will set you free
as you come to Me

Insight:

The New Hampshire State Motto is "Live free or die". For the believer in the Lord Jesus Christ, we "die" to self and come "alive" in Christ. Since it is for freedom that Christ died for us, we should live in this freedom. The difference between fact and truth must be understood, e.g. it may be a fact that you do not believe in Christ as Savior of your soul, but that does not change the truth of His Word, the Bible. The Word is clear on how we should live to have true freedom in our life.

Your Thoughts:

GOD'S PLAN FOR A HAPPY MARRIAGE

Since God ordained marriage let us see what He says about it in His Word.
Following these scriptures will help assure a good and happy marriage.

Genesis 2:24 (NIV)
Vs.24 That is why a man leaves his father and mother and is united to his wife, and they become one flesh.

This is foundational of married relationship, husband and wife forsaking all else to live with one another.

Committed in marriage means that the most important duty of both husband and wife is to put the other first in the beginning of marriage so as to establish a unique relationship as the marriage progresses. This will help you learn of each other's desires and thoughts.

Hebrews 13:4 NIV
Marriage should be honored by all, and the marriage bed kept pure, for God will judge the adulterer and all the sexually immoral.

This is so important, for the intimacy in the marriage goes beyond the physical, but involves the emotions, spirit, mind and soul of each. Disharmony in marriage over a number of issues often leading to divorce in marriages.

1 Corinthians 7:1-7 NIV
Now for the matters you wrote about: "It is good for a man not to have sexual relations with a woman." 2 But since sexual immorality is occurring, each man should have sexual relations with his own wife, and each woman with her own husband. 3 The husband should fulfill his marital duty to his wife, and likewise the wife to her husband. 4 The wife does not have authority over her own body but yields it to her husband. In the same way, the husband does not have authority over his own body but yields it to his wife. 5 Do not deprive each other except perhaps by mutual consent and for a time, so that you may devote yourselves to prayer. Then come together again so that Satan will not tempt you because of your lack of self-control. 6 I say this as a concession, not as a command. 7 I wish that all of you were as I am. But each of you has your own gift from God; one has this gift, another has that.

These should be the priorities in your marriage:
First, is your relationship with God, separately and individually. Pray together regularly.

Second, is family.

Third, is work, profession,

When these are out of order, problems will arise and the enemy of your soul will be at your door. You will know because you will not have peace in your life.

1 Peter 3:1-7 NIV
1 WIVES, in the same way submit yourselves to your own husbands so that, if any of them do not believe the word, they may be won over without words by the behavior of their wives, 2 when they see the purity and reverence of your lives. 3 Your beauty should not come from outward adornment, such as elaborate hairstyles and the wearing of gold jewelry or fine clothes. 4 Rather, it should be that of your inner self, the unfading beauty of a gentle and quiet spirit, which is of great worth in God's sight. 5 For this is the way the holy women of the past who put their hope in God used to adorn themselves. They submitted themselves to their own husbands, 6 like Sarah, who obeyed Abraham and called him her lord. You are her daughters if you do what is right and do not give way to fear.

7 HUSBANDS, in the same way be considerate as you live with your wives, and treat them with respect as the weaker partner and as heirs with you of the gracious gift of life, so that nothing will hinder your prayers.

These scriptures verses are self-explanatory.

Submission to one another is foundational in a good and happy relationship.

A FAMILY THAT PRAYS TOGETHER STAYS TOGETHER.
Happy wife, happy life!

Some scriptures to encourage you.

John13:34"CEV But I am giving you a new command. You must love each other, just as I have loved you

1 Peter1:22 ERV You have made yourselves pure by obeying the truth. Now you can have true love for your brothers and sisters. So love each other deeply—with all your heart.

1 Peter 3:8 MEV Finally, be all of one mind be loving toward one another, be gracious and be kind.

Memory verse 1 Corinthians 16:14 CEV
Show love in everything you do.

Rhyme Time
Two are better than one
When you worship the Son

Insights:

Good communication is important in any relationship, learn and practice on listening to each other.

    A. Put God first in your marriage.
    B. Go to the Word of God for answers. Ask yourself. "What would Jesus do?"
    C. Make your marriage a personal commitment to one another daily!
    D. Seek godly counsel when needed.

Your Thoughts:

PRINCIPLES OF SOWING & REAPING

Today's devotion is on "The law of sowing and reaping".
Do not be fooled: You cannot cheat God. People harvest only what they plant."
Galatians 6:7 NCV

A farmer planting corn expects to reap com; This principle of sowing and reaping also applies to every person, both in our private and professional lives. It does not matter what your belief system is, the effects of this law are always at work. It is a natural and a spiritual law.

How many people have shown sorrow or grief because of wrong actions, wishing they could change the outcome. Think of those in prison and bad relationships. Conversely one whose actions are always proper will rejoice in the good harvest yielded.

It is the duty of all of us to live life that will produce a good harvest, underwritten with good morals and ethical integrity, you can expect results that will bless you and not do harm to others.

The fruit of your labor will be evident to all, as to whether or not they were "sown" with good seed.

Morals count, Faith matters.

May the Lord guide you as you sow good seed in all that you do and say. May God bless you with a great harvest.

Memory Verse Proverbs 11:18 CEV
Meanness gets you nowhere, but goodness is rewarded.

Rhyme Time:
Good seed sown results in good harvest
This will benefit most people the greatest

Insight:

All of us in our daily lives, with our words and actions, determine if we will be a blessing or a curse to others.

"A word fitly spoken is like apples of gold in settings of silver,". Proverbs 25:11 MEV

Your Thoughts:

PLAN YOUR DESTINY

1. God has a plan for your life (destiny, calling) ESV unless noted.
   Jeremiah 29:11-13 "For I know the plans I have for you, declares the LORD, plans for welfare[a] and not for evil, to give you a future and a hope. [12] Then you will call upon me and come and pray to me, and I will hear you. [13] You will seek me and find me, when you seek me with all your heart.

   Jeremiah 33:3 'Call to me and I will answer you, and will tell you great and hidden things that you have not known."

   God's phone number!
   In Exodus 26:30 God instructs Moses on building the Tabernacle in exact detail. Temple built according to God's plan we are the tabernacle (temple) of God.1 Corinthians 3:16

2. God will help you complete the plan.
   Proverbs 3:5-8
   Proverbs 15:22 Plans foil for lack of counsel.
   Proverbs 16:3 Commit to the Lord whatever you do and He will establish your plans
   Proverbs 20:18 Plans are established by seeking advice; so if you wage war, obtain guidance.
   Psalms 37:1-6 Don't fret, trust God, delight in the Lord, commit your way to the Lord.

3. Live in accordance with His plan.
   Matthew 7:21 -23 Will of God paramount
   Galatians 5:16-26 Natural man versus spiritual man
   2 Peter 1:5-11 Be sure of your purpose in life.
   Proverbs 3:1-6 Trust God and not on your own understanding
   Acts 10:34-35 God does not show favoritism.

Use the planning chart to track your progress of important activities.

Memory Verse John 10:10
The thief comes only to steal and kill and destroy.
I came that they may have life and have it abundantly.

Rhyme Time
A good planning chart
Will bless your heart

Insight:

Start today on the path you should take according to God's plan for your life. As savings wisely invested grow, guess how much more will be the investment in God's plan for you grow in this life.

Your Thoughts:

PLANNING CHART

A   Military | |
C   Marriage | |
T   Career | |
I   Work | |
V   Business | |
I   Educationl | |
T   Training | |
Y   Others | |
    Bible Study | |
    Ministry | |

0

Timeline Milestones
Weeks/ Months/ Years

POWER OF THREE "GOD'S KNOT"

Ecclesiastes 4:9-12 NLT

9 Two people are better off than one, for they can help each other succeed. 10 If one person falls, the other can reach out and help. But someone who falls alone is in real trouble. 11 Likewise, two people lying close together can keep each other warm. But how can one be warm alone? 12 A person standing alone can be attacked and defeated, but two can stand back-to-back and conquer. Three are even better, for a triple-braided cord is not easily broken. New living translation

The actual Hebrew does not say "three strands" but simply "three." The Hebrew word that is translated as "three stands" is *msullas* and it means "three." Meaning that three smaller cords are twisted together for greater strength. Three smaller cords twisted together are better than one or two smaller cords by themselves.

A. RULE OF THREE / Examples
    Real estate: *Location, Location, Location*

    1. "Veni, vidi, vici" (to come, to see, to conquer) Julius Caesar
    2. *"Duty, Honor, Country".* General Patton, West Point 1962
    3. "Life, liberty, and the pursuit of happiness– the American Declaration of Independence.
    4. Accused, convicted, punished / accused, acquitted, freed.
    5. Hook, line, and sinker, Fuel, Oxygen, ignition, Lock, stock, barrel, Water, ice, steam,
    6. Hydrogen, hydrogen, oxygen = H20 = water,
    7. Mother, father, child,
    8. Love Faith, Hope

B. Rule of three to teach survival:
    a. 3 minutes without air.
    b. 3 days without water.
    c. 3 weeks without food,
    d. 3 months without hope.

Time consist of three Phases; past, presence, future.
Man's existence is also threefold- Body, mind and spirit,

Number 3 biblical meaning:
The number 3 is used 467 times in the Bible. It pictures completeness, though to a lesser degree than 7. The meaning of this number derives from the fact that it is the first of four spiritually perfect numerals (the others being 7 the number of completion: Seven

churches, seven seals, seven horns, seven trumpets. 10 the number of completion: ten Commandments, in Revelation – world's activity Chapters13 and 17 and 12 the number of final perfection: Twelve gate of Jerusalem, 12 Hebrew tribes, 12 Apostles.)

The 3 righteous patriarchs before the flood were Abel, Enoch and Noah. After the deluge there were three righteous "fathers", Abraham, Isaac and Jacob (later renamed Israel).

There are 27 books in the New Testament, which is 3x3x3, or completeness to the third power.

Jesus prayed three times in the Garden of Gethsemane before His arrest.
He was placed on the cross at the 3rd hour of the day (9 am.) and died at the 9th hour (3 pm.). There were 3 hours of darkness that covered the land while Jesus was suffering on the cross from the 6th hour to the 9th hour. Three is the number of resurrection. Christ was dead for three days

C. These example are interdependent and function together.
1. Father, Son and Holy Spirit "God's Knot"
2. past, present, future
3. Body, mind, soul/spirit
4. Sun, Moon, Earth
5. Your prayer, inspired by the Holy Spirit and Christ interceding at the right hand of God.

In our natural life we need healthy body, sound mind, and right spirit to function best.

Three attitudes God always favors.
1. Holiness. Be Holy Leviticus 19:2,7:6, Exodus. 22:31, 1 Peter 1:15,16,
2. Believe God's word Isaiah 43:10, John 14:11-14.
3. Obey. Take action, be a doer of the word. James 1:22.

Memory Verse Ecclesiastes 4:12b ESV
a threefold cord is not quickly broken.

Rhyme Time
A cord of three strands
Will be your helping hand

Insight:

The Father, Son and Holy Spirit (Super power of three) are always with the believer in Christ. All working together for our blessings. This understanding should be foremost in our minds and hearts. We pray to the Father (God), Inspired by the Holy Spirit, in the name of Jesus.

Your thoughts:

A WAY OUT OF TEMPTATION

Those who are believers in Christ are a new creation.

Ephesians 4:22-24 NLT
22 throw off your old sinful nature and your former way of life, which- is corrupted by lust and deception. 23 Instead, let the Spirit renew your thoughts and attitudes. 24 Put on your new nature, created to be like God—truly righteous and holy.

Galatians 6:15 NLT
It doesn't matter whether we have been circumcised or not. What counts is whether we have been transformed into a new creation.

2 Corinthians 5:17 (NKJV)
17 Therefore, if anyone *is* in Christ, *he is* a new creation; old things have passed away; behold, all things have become new.

God shows us in His word, as born- again believers, how we can overcome temptations. A window of opportunity to find a way out.

1 Corinthians 10:12-13 (NLT)
12 If you think you are standing strong, be careful not to fall. 13 The temptations in your life are no different from what others experience. And God is faithful. He will not allow the temptation to be more than you can stand. When you are tempted, he will show you a way out so that you can endure. (overcome)

Look at the four stages and see how this can happen.

Stage 1	Temptation overcame you.
Stage 2	Shows a way out of temptation, dotted curve
Stage 3	You overcame temptation, solid curve
Stage 4	Replace old behavior with new behavior

Putting Off the Old Self/Putting On the New Self
Stage 1   Ephesians 4:22-24

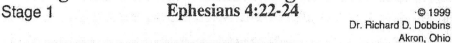
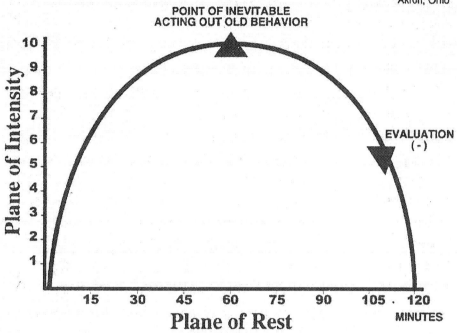

Putting Off the Old Self/Putting On the New Self
Stage 2   Ephesians 4:22-24

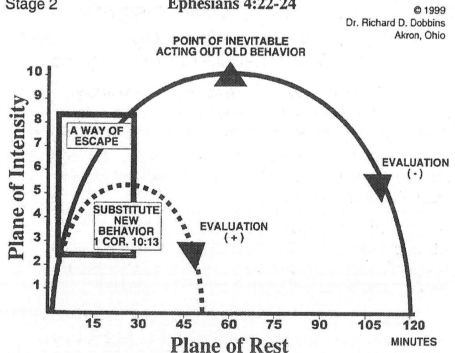

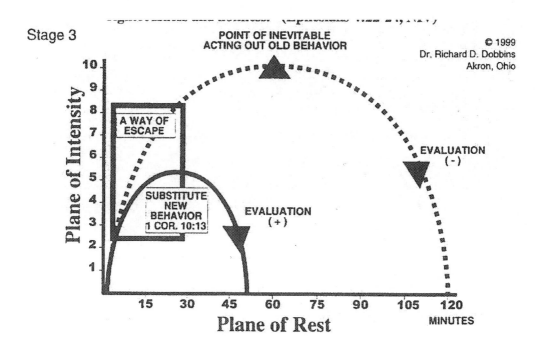

Putting Off the Old Self/Putting On the New Self
Ephesians 4:22-24

Stage 4

© 1999
Dr. Richard D. Dobbins
Akron, Ohio

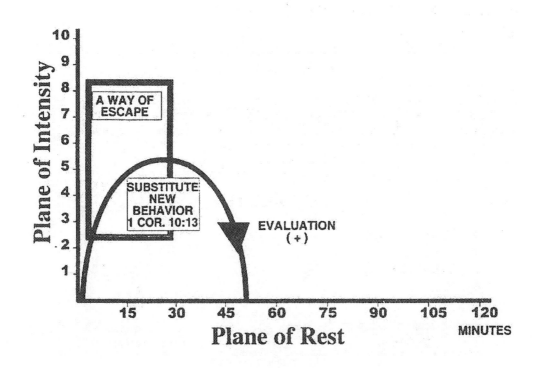

Memory Verse 1 Corinthians 10:13b NLV
But when you are tempted, He will make a way for you to keep from falling into sin.

Rhyme Time
When tempted by sin
Change course of action to win

Insight:

Temptation is before everyone. Some will use different ways to avoid it, ignore it and even rationalize it. Sometimes people will say "the devil made me do it". Not so for the believer in Jesus Christ. Thanks to the Word of God, Dr. Dobbins shows us a way of escape from temptation. This in the power of the Spirit, using God's Word! As a new creation in Christ we now can adopt new behavior in our life.

Your Thoughts:

POWER OF PRAYER

James 5:16 Amplified Bible (AMP)

16 Confess *your* trespasses to one another, and pray for one another, that you may be healed. The effective, fervent prayer of a righteous man avails much.

Fervent means having *passionate intensity!*

Prayer of the righteous: read Proverbs Chapters 10 and 11

Bring them near to God
Open way to Spirit Filled life
Bring them power for ministry
Build them up spiritually
Give them insight into Christ's provision for them
Help them overcome Satan
Clarify God's will for them
Enable them to receive spiritual gifts
Bring then into fellowship with God
Bring them grace, mercy and peace
Bring the lost to Christ
Bring them the wisdom, revelation and knowledge of Christ
Bring them deliverance from trouble
Glorify God with peace and thanksgiving
Make Christ's presence real to them
Ensure them of their final salvation and of Christ's intercession

Memory Verse ESV Matthew 7:7-8
"Ask, and it will be given to you; seek, and you will
find; knock, and it will be opened to you.

Rhyme Time
No prayer, No power
Know prayer, Know power

Your Thoughts:

BENEFITS OF TRUSTING GOD

Proverbs 3:1-8 NKJV

Vs 1 My son, do not forget my law, But let your heart keep my commands; 2 For length of days and long life and peace they will add to you.

Vs 1,2 connect keeping His commandments with a full productive, prosperous, long and peaceful life.

His law, teaching, precepts, decrees, commands and statutes as they apply to our life are not to be forgotten or forsaken. Look up Psalm 119 and underline all those words. Take time to understand how they impact your life.

Remember (2 Cor. 1:20) AMP. For as many as are the promises of God, in Christ they are [all answered] "Yes." So through Him we say our "Amen" to the glory of God.

Vs 3 Let not mercy and truth forsake you; Bind them around your neck, Write them on the tablet of your heart.

Our attitude and heart must be merciful and kind (closing all hatred and selfishness from entering in), and truthful (stopping all hypocrisy or falsehood). Holding them in your heart, becoming part of your inner self. This results in having favor, clear understanding and being honored by God and man.

Vs 4 And so find favor and high esteem In the sight of God and man.

This comes about not by our promoting ourselves but being recognized by God and others.

Vs 5 Trust in the Lord with all your heart, And lean not on your own understanding.

Do not default to human or natural understanding in anything you do. Then He will show the path to your destiny.

Vs 6 In all your ways acknowledge Him, And He shall direct your paths.

This does not mean to abandon common sense but to seek and wait upon God's timing and wisdom. (Wisdom is comprehensive insight into His way and purpose for you.)

Vs 7 Do not be wise in your own eyes; Fear the Lord and depart from evil.

It is important to continually fear and worship the Lord, always turning your back on thoughts away from things that are evil, unrighteous, not of God.

Vs 8 It will be health to your flesh, And strength to your bones.

Obedience of above will produce health and wellness and abundant life that Jesus tells us in John 10:10

Memory Vs Proverbs 3:5 MEV
Trust in the Lord with all your heart
And lean not on your own understanding

Rhyme Time
When we keep God away
Our plans will go astray

Insight:

Seek and wait has to do with His presence and timing. Remember God is always on time, since He is Omniscient (all knowing) nothing is hidden from Him. He knows the beginning to the end of every situation! Trust Him.

Your Thoughts:

ARE YOU READY?

Marjorie M. Couture
April 17, 1998

Men of God where are you
In this harvest time
Don't you know that you
Are part of His design
The highways and byways, marketplace
And yes, the church
Need men of God to reach the lost
All those who hurt.

Are you ready, are you going to do His Will
He's chosen you, His plan to fulfill
The time is now, tomorrow may be too late
To bring in the sheep, show them the gate

You are the witness
The salt and the light
Put on your armor
And join in the fight
The enemy isn't waiting
He comes to destroy
So tell them of Jesus
He'll fill them with joy

SECTION 4

FAITH MATTERS

These are recorded events of people being healed through faith in God.

THE LORD'S COVENANT PROMISE TO ABRAM

Genesis 15:1-6 (NLT)

1 Sometime later, the LORD spoke to Abram in a vision and said to him, "Do not be afraid, Abram, for I will protect you, and your reward will be great."

[2] But Abram replied, "O Sovereign LORD, what good are all your blessings when I don't even have a son? Since you've given me no children, Eliezer of Damascus, a servant in my household, will inherit all my wealth. [3] You have given me no descendants of my own, so one of my servants will be my heir."

[4] Then the LORD said to him, "No, your servant will not be your heir, for you will have a son of your own who will be your heir." [5] Then the LORD took Abram outside and said to him, "Look up into the sky and count the stars if you can. That's how many descendants you will have!" 6 And Abram believed the LORD, and the LORD counted him as righteous because of his faith.

Insight:

God gave Abram who was in despair a vision of encouragement and protection, and to provide an heir to all he owned.

Abram believed God and was considered righteous (right standing with God) because of Abram's faith in God promise.

The Lord can speak to anyone through a vision, a thought, a sign, or any other form of communication.

Regarding faith we read Romans 10:16-18 (ERV)[16] But not all the people accepted that good news. Isaiah said, "Lord, who believed what we told them?"[a] [17] So faith comes from hearing the Good News. And people hear the Good News when someone tells them about Christ.

H.E.A.R.
   Hear the word.
      Everyday.
         Accept the word.
            Respond in faith.

Your Thoughts:

THE FAITH OF A ROMAN OFFICER

Matthew 8:5-13 NLT

⁵ When Jesus returned to Capernaum, a Roman officer came and pleaded with him, ⁶ "Lord, my young servant[c] lies in bed, paralyzed and in terrible pain." ⁷ Jesus said, "I will come and heal him."

⁸ But the officer said, "Lord, I am not worthy to have you come into my home. Just say the word from where you are, and my servant will be healed. ⁹ I know this because I am under the authority of my superior officers, and I have authority over my soldiers. I only need to say, 'Go,' and they go, or 'Come,' and they come. And if I say to my slaves, 'Do this,' they do it."

¹⁰ When Jesus heard this, he was amazed. Turning to those who were following him, he said, "I tell you the truth, I haven't seen faith like this in all Israel! ¹¹ And I tell you this, that many Gentiles will come from all over the world—from east and west—and sit down with Abraham, Isaac, and Jacob at the feast in the Kingdom of Heaven. ¹² But many Israelites—those for whom the Kingdom was prepared—will be thrown into outer darkness, where there will be weeping and gnashing of teeth."

¹³ Then Jesus said to the Roman officer, "Go back home. Because you believed, it has happened." And the young servant was healed that same hour.

Insight:

This man came to Jesus begging him to heal his servant who was in great pain. Jesus said He would come! The man felt unworthy for Jesus to enter house and as an Officer is a man who had authority over others and was under authority. He recognized that he only had to obey orders and give orders without being present. Realized the authority Jesus commanded. Jesus could just command the healing where he was. He did and the servant was healed the same hour. Jesus was surprised, amazed of the Officer's faith.

Will Jesus be amazed at your faith in Him?
Humbleness must always be in our attitude in seeking God's favor. James 4:10
When you pray believe in faith that God hears your prayers and knows when and how to answer them

Let faith in God increase in all we say and do.

Your Thoughts:

OLD TESTAMENT: ABRAHAM TESTED

Genesis 22:1-14 (NIV)

22 Sometime later God tested Abraham. He said to him, "Abraham!" "Here I am," he replied. [2] Then God said, "Take your son, your only son, whom you love—Isaac—and go to the region of Moriah. Sacrifice him there as a burnt offering on a mountain I will show you."

[3] Early the next morning Abraham got up and loaded his donkey. He took with him two of his servants and his son Isaac. When he had cut enough wood for the burnt offering, he set out for the place God had told him about. [4] On the third day Abraham looked up and saw the place in the distance. [5] He said to his servants, "Stay here with the donkey while I and the boy go over there. We will worship and then we will come back to you."

[6] Abraham took the wood for the burnt offering and placed it on his son Isaac, and he himself carried the fire and the knife. As the two of them went on together, [7] Isaac spoke up and said to his father Abraham, "Father?" "Yes, my son?" Abraham replied. "The fire and wood are here," Isaac said, "but where is the lamb for the burnt offering?"

[8] Abraham answered, "God himself will provide the lamb for the burnt offering, my son." And the two of them went on together.

[9] When they reached the place God had told him about, Abraham built an altar there and arranged the wood on it. He bound his son Isaac and laid him on the altar, on top of the wood. [10] Then he reached out his hand and took the knife to slay his son. [11] But the angel of the Lord called out to him from heaven, "Abraham! Abraham!" "Here I am," he replied.

[12] "Do not lay a hand on the boy," he said. "Do not do anything to him. Now I know that you fear God, because you have not withheld from me your son, your only son."

[13] Abraham looked up and there in a thicket he saw a ram[a] caught by its horns. He went over and took the ram and sacrificed it as a burnt offering instead of his son. [14] So Abraham called that place The Lord Will Provide. And to this day it is said, "On the mountain of the Lord it will be provided."

Insight:

Abraham was tested and found faithful again, remember when he was called Abram In Genesis 15:1-6 he was faithful then also. It is very much important to have faith in God mainly when it involves you personally. We are tested and tempted everyday of our life as believers in Christ by Satan, demons, people, situations, religious people, government and the list go on.

Be certain that God always reward the righteous! Living by faith in God is believing His Word and apply it to your life. Believing is being faithful.

Hebrews 11:6 NIV [6] And without faith it is impossible to please God, because anyone who comes to him must believe that he exists and that he rewards those who earnestly seek him.

Three reasons for not having faith.

1. We don't know God.
2. We don't believe God
3. We don't trust God

If any of these you are having problem with confess it now, repent and believe in God for salvation through His Son, Jesus Christ.

Your thoughts:

NEW TESTAMENT: JESUS FORGIVES AND HEALS A PARALYZED MAN

Matthew 9:1-8 NIV

9 Jesus stepped into a boat, crossed over and came to his own town. [2] Some men brought to him a paralyzed man, lying on a mat. When Jesus saw their faith, he said to the man, "Take heart, son; your sins are forgiven." [3] At this, some of the teachers of the law said to themselves, "This fellow is blaspheming!"[4] Knowing their thoughts, Jesus said, "Why do you entertain evil thoughts in your hearts? [5] Which is easier: to say, 'Your sins are forgiven,' or to say, 'Get up and walk'? [6] But I want you to know that the Son of Man has authority on earth to forgive sins." So, he said to the paralyzed man, "Get up, take your mat and go home." [7] Then the man got up and went home. [8] When the crowd saw this, they were filled with awe; and they praised God, who had given such authority to man.

Insight:

When Christ sees faith in you, He sends blessings, healings, miracles and many things we can only imagine or think.

Ephesians 3:20 NKJV
[20] Now to Him who is able to do exceedingly abundantly above all that we ask or think, according to the power that works in us

Your Faith is the connection between believing and things happening. Let faith arise in you and God's enemies be scattered!

Your Thoughts:

VICTORY OVER THE AMALEKITES

Exodus 17:8-13 NKJV

[8] Now Amalek came and fought with Israel in Rephidim. [9] And Moses said to Joshua, "Choose us some men and go out, fight with Amalek. Tomorrow I will stand on the top of the hill with the rod of God in my hand." [10] So Joshua did as Moses said to him, and fought with Amalek. And Moses, Aaron, and Hur went up to the top of the hill. [11] And so it was, when Moses held up his hand, that Israel prevailed; and when he let down his hand, Amalek prevailed. [12] But Moses' hands became [a]heavy; so they took a stone and put it under him, and he sat on it. And Aaron and Hur supported his hands, one on one side, and the other on the other side; and his hands were steady until the going down of the sun. [13] So Joshua defeated Amalek and his people with the edge of the sword.

Insight:

The Amalekites were a formidable tribe of nomads living in the area south of Canaan, between Mount Seir and the Egyptian border

The Amalekites, descendants of Amalek, were an ancient biblical nation living near the land of Canaan. They were the first nation to attack the Jewish people after the Exodus from Egypt, and they are seen as the archetypal enemy of the Jews. Relentless enemies of Israel

Here is a story of how God used events and people to accomplish His will.
Moses sought the Lord in this time of peril. During the battle Moses looked over the battle scene and in arms raised up praised God. Aaron and Hur were used to aid Moses. God always provides someone when we need help to do His work.

Praising God in all situations is God's will for you in Jesus Christ. 1 Thessalonians 5:18
Matthew Chapter 9 continues to show the miracles of Jesus. He also commented on their faith as key to His healings.

A GIRL RESTORED TO LIFE AND A WOMAN HEALED

Matthew 9:18-26 NKJV

18 While He spoke these things to them, behold, a ruler came and worshiped Him, saying, "My daughter has just died, but come and lay Your hand on her and she will live." 19 So Jesus arose and followed him, and so did His disciples.

20 And suddenly, a woman who had a flow of blood for twelve years came from behind and touched the hem of His garment. 21 For she said to herself, "If only I may touch His garment, I shall be made well." 22 But Jesus turned around, and when He saw her, He said, "Be of good cheer, daughter; your faith has made you well." And the woman was made well from that hour.

23 When Jesus came into the ruler's house, and saw the flute players and the noisy crowd wailing, 24 He said to them, "Make room, for the girl is not dead, but sleeping."

And they ridiculed Him. 25 But when the crowd was put outside, He went in and took her by the hand, and the girl arose. 26 And the report of this went out into all that land.

Matthew 9:28-32 NKJV
Two Blind Men Healed
"Son of David, have mercy on us!"

28 And when He had come into the house, the blind men came to Him. And Jesus said to them, "Do you believe that I am able to do this?" They said to Him, "Yes, Lord."

29 Then He touched their eyes, saying, "According to your faith let it be to you." 30 And their eyes were opened. And Jesus sternly warned them, saying, "See that no one knows it." 31 But when they had departed, they spread the news about Him in all that country.

A Mute Man Speaks
32 As they went out, behold, they brought to Him a man, mute and demon-possessed. 33 And when the demon was cast out, the mute spoke. And the multitudes marveled, saying, "It was never seen like this in Israel!"

Insights:

All of these miracle and healings were done to people who believed and had faith that Jesus could heal them. What level of faith do you have in Jesus for your healings? Jesus has given these gifts of the Holy Spirit to believers today. See 1 Corinthians Chapter 12 and 14.

Hebrews 11:1 (ESV) Now faith is the assurance of things hoped for, the conviction of things not seen.

Can you define your faith in Christ?

Your Thoughts:

CROSSING THE JORDAN RIVER

Joshua 3-:1-17 NIV

In chapter 1, God tells Joshua, Moses is dead, you Joshua will cross the Jordan and God will be with you in all of it. In vs 9 God commanded him to be strong and courageous, The Lord your God will be with you wherever you go.

Crossing the Jordan River Read Joshua chapter 3 NIV
Early in the morning Joshua and all the Israelites set out from Shittim and went to the Jordan, where they camped before crossing over. ² After three days the officers went throughout the camp, ³ giving orders to the people: "When you see the ark of the covenant of the LORD your God, and the Levitical priests carrying it, you are to move out from your positions and follow it. ⁴ Then you will know which way to go, since you have never been this way before. But keep a distance of about two thousand cubits[a] between you and the ark; do not go near it."

⁵ Joshua told the people, "Consecrate yourselves, for tomorrow the LORD will do amazing things among you."

⁶ Joshua said to the priests, "Take up the ark of the covenant and pass on ahead of the people." So, they took it up and went ahead of them.

⁷ And the LORD said to Joshua, "Today I will begin to exalt you in the eyes of all Israel, so they may know that I am with you as I was with Moses. ⁸ Tell the priests who carry the ark of the covenant: 'When you reach the edge of the Jordan's waters, go and stand in the river.'"

⁹ Joshua said to the Israelites, "Come here and listen to the words of the LORD your God. ¹⁰ This is how you will know that the living God is among you and that he will certainly drive out before you the Canaanites, Hittites, Hivites, Perizzites, Girgashites, Amorites and Jebusites. ¹¹ See, the ark of the covenant of the Lord of all the earth will go into the Jordan ahead of you. ¹² Now then, choose twelve men from the tribes of Israel, one from each tribe. ¹³ And as soon as the priests who carry the ark of the LORD—the Lord of all the earth—set foot in the Jordan, its waters flowing downstream will be cut off and stand up in a heap."

¹⁴ So when the people broke camp to cross the Jordan, the priests carrying the ark of the covenant went ahead of them. ¹⁵ Now the Jordan is at flood stage all during harvest. Yet as soon as the priests who carried the ark reached the Jordan and their feet touched the water's edge, ¹⁶ the water from upstream stopped flowing. It piled up in a heap a great distance away, at a town called Adam in the vicinity of Zarethan, while the water flowing down to the Sea of the Arabah (that is, the Dead Sea) was completely cut off. So, the people crossed over opposite Jericho. ¹⁷ The priests who carried the ark of the covenant of the LORD stopped in the middle

of the Jordan and stood on dry ground, while all Israel passed by until the whole nation had completed the crossing on dry ground.

Insight:

God called Joshua to take the Israelites across the Jordan River. This was a strong testimony of the miraculous work of God so all people and tribes would know this miraculous crossing affirmed God's presence with them and His promise to remove their enemies from the land. The miracle was done "so that all the peoples of the earth might know that the hand of the Lord is powerful." No other god could compare in power.

God uses those who believe the things God said He would do. The bible is full of God's promises to the faithful and righteous people in Christ.

The details of the crossing of the Israelites on parted waters when it was at flood stage and on dry land is impossible with man. The faith of Joshua to obey and follow God as he did Moses before are reasons that God blessed the nation with these miracles. Today we have enemies of Christ in the land. As Joshua did, we also must be faithful to what God has called each of us to do.

This is no small matter as the scriptures declare in Matthew 6:33 NKJV "But seek first his kingdom and his righteousness, and all these things will be given to you as well".

Hebrews 13:8. Jesus Christ is the same yesterday and today and forever.

Are you trusting and obeying His commands and teachings? We are given eternal life in Christ, let us continue to praise and worship Him in this temporal life. For his blessings are manifold and eternal.

Your Thoughts:

JESUS DRIVES OUT DEMONS

Matthew 9:32-33 NIV

32 While they were going out, a man who was demon-possessed and could not talk was brought to Jesus. 33 And when the demon was driven out, the man who had been mute spoke. The crowd was amazed and said, "Nothing like this has ever been seen in Israel.

Matthew 17:14-21 NIV

14 When they came to the crowd, a man approached Jesus and knelt before him. 15 "Lord, have mercy on my son," he said. "He has seizures and is suffering greatly. He often falls into the fire or into the water. 16 I brought him to your disciples, but they could not heal him."

17 "You unbelieving and pervs generation," Jesus replied, "how long shall I stay with you? How long shall I put up with you? Bring the boy here to me." 18 Jesus rebuked the demon, and it came out of the boy, and he was healed at that moment. 19 Then the disciples came to Jesus in private and asked, "Why couldn't we drive it out?"

20 He replied, "Because you have so little faith. Truly I tell you, if you have faith as small as a mustard seed, you can say to this mountain, 'Move from here to there,' and it will move. Nothing will be impossible for you." 21 [a]However, this kind does not go out except by prayer and fasting."

Faith Without Works Is Dead

James 2:14-26 NKJV

14 What *does it* profit, my brethren, if someone says he has faith but does not have works? Can faith save him? 15 If a brother or sister is naked and destitute of daily food, 16 and one of you says to them, "Depart in peace, be warmed and filled," but you do not give them the things which are needed for the body, what *does it* profit? 17 Thus also faith by itself, if it does not have works, is dead.

18 But someone will say, "You have faith, and I have works." Show me your faith without [a]your works, and I will show you my faith by [b]my works. 19 You believe that there is one God. You do well. Even the demons believe—and tremble! 20 But do you want to know, O foolish man, that faith without works is [c]dead? 21 Was not Abraham our father justified by works when he offered Isaac his son on the altar? 22 Do you see that faith was working together with his works, and by works faith was made [d]perfect? 23 And the Scripture was fulfilled which says, "Abraham believed God, and it was [e]accounted to him for righteousness." And he was called the friend of God. 24 You see then that a man is justified by works, and not by faith only. 25 Likewise, was not Rahab the harlot also justified by works when she received the messengers

and sent them out another way? [26] For as the body without the spirit is dead, so faith without works is dead also.

Insight:

Jesus went about healing all and chastised the disciples because of their little faith. The Disciples and believers then and today have the same Holy Spirit in them. The Lord expects Christians today to serve people in the power of God. Faith in Christ is built upon the Word of God, the bible, the Work of God through the Holy Spirit in us, and our obedience to God.

As works without faith is dead, let us do His work with increasing faith. Let us pray and fast and see God's mighty miracles happen!

Your Thoughts:

GIDEON DEFEATS THE MIDIANITES

Judges 7:1-25 NIV

1 Early in the morning, Jerub-Baal (that is, Gideon) and all his men camped at the spring of Harod. The camp of Midian was north of them in the valley near the hill of Moreh. ² The LORD said to Gideon, "You have too many men. I cannot deliver Midian into their hands, or Israel would boast against me, 'My own strength has saved me.' ³ Now announce to the army, 'Anyone who trembles with fear may turn back and leave Mount Gilead.'" So twenty-two thousand men left, while ten thousand remained.

⁴ But the LORD said to Gideon, "There are still too many men. Take them down to the water, and I will thin them out for you there. If I say, 'This one shall go with you,' he shall go; but if I say, 'This one shall not go with you,' he shall not go."

⁵ So Gideon took the men down to the water. There the LORD told him, "Separate those who lap the water with their tongues as a dog laps from those who kneel down to drink." ⁶ Three hundred of them drank from cupped hands, lapping like dogs. All the rest got down on their knees to drink.

⁷ The LORD said to Gideon, "With the three hundred men that lapped I will save you and give the Midianites into your hands. Let all the others go home." ⁸ So Gideon sent the rest of the Israelites home but kept the three hundred, who took over the provisions and trumpets of the others.

Now the camp of Midian lay below him in the valley. ⁹ During that night the LORD said to Gideon, "Get up, go down against the camp, because I am going to give it into your hands. ¹⁰ If you are afraid to attack, go down to the camp with your servant Purah ¹¹ and listen to what they are saying. Afterward, you will be encouraged to attack the camp." So he and Purah his servant went down to the outposts of the camp. ¹² The Midianites, the Amalekites and all the other eastern peoples had settled in the valley, thick as locusts. Their camels could no more be counted than the sand on the seashore.

¹³ Gideon arrived just as a man was telling a friend his dream. "I had a dream," he was saying. "A round loaf of barley bread came tumbling into the Midianite camp. It struck the tent with such force that the tent overturned and collapsed."

¹⁴ His friend responded, "This can be nothing other than the sword of Gideon son of Joash, the Israelite. God has given the Midianites and the whole camp into his hands."

[15] When Gideon heard the dream and its interpretation, he bowed down and worshiped. He returned to the camp of Israel and called out, "Get up! The LORD has given the Midianite camp into your hands." [16] Dividing the three hundred men into three companies, he placed trumpets and empty jars in the hands of all of them, with torches inside.

[17] "Watch me," he told them. "Follow my lead. When I get to the edge of the camp, do exactly as I do. [18] When I and all who are with me blow our trumpets, then from all around the camp blow yours and shout, 'For the LORD and for Gideon.'"

[19] Gideon and the hundred men with him reached the edge of the camp at the beginning of the middle watch, just after they had changed the guard. They blew their trumpets and broke the jars that were in their hands. [20] The three companies blew the trumpets and smashed the jars. Grasping the torches in their left hands and holding in their right hands the trumpets they were to blow, they shouted, "A sword for the LORD and for Gideon!" [21] While each man held his position around the camp, all the Midianites ran, crying out as they fled.

[22] When the three hundred trumpets sounded, the LORD caused the men throughout the camp to turn on each other with their swords. The army fled to Beth Shittah toward Zererah as far as the border of Abel Meholah near Tabbath. [23] Israelites from Naphtali, Asher and all Manasseh were called out, and they pursued the Midianites. [24] Gideon sent messengers throughout the hill country of Ephraim, saying, "Come down against the Midianites and seize the waters of the Jordan ahead of them as far as Beth Barah." So all the men of Ephraim were called out and they seized the waters of the Jordan as far as Beth Barah. [25] They also captured two of the Midianite leaders, Oreb and Zeeb. They killed Oreb at the rock of Oreb, and Zeeb at the winepress of Zeeb. They pursued the Midianites and brought the heads of Oreb and Zeeb to Gideon, who was by the Jordan.

Insight:

This account in the bible tells of God's detailed instructions on having victory over your enemies. Even when Gideon had a large army of 32000 men, the Lord who wanted to receive the glory used only 300, less than 10%, vs 1-8.

Isaiah 55:8 NIV "For my thoughts are not your thoughts, neither are your ways my ways," declares the Lord.

The Israelites again were facing armies that wanted to destroy them.

Gideon interpreted a dream as to what he must do with the 300 men against an army too numerous to count. Vs 9-14. Gideon now had a strategy on how to defeat the enemy vs 15-25. It never matters the size of your enemies, temptations, oppression, persecutions, rejections, struggles. God is able to do more than we can think or imagine. Ephesians 3:20. Often, we find our self alone in the battle, remember the battle is the Lord's. Call upon Him in this hour of need and above all praise Him in all situations. There is Holy Spirit power in praising God. Make it part of your devotions today. After all we are to live by faith!

Your Thoughts:

JESUS HEALS THE BLIND

Matthew 9:27-30 (AMP)

[27] As Jesus went on from there, two blind men followed Him, screaming loudly, "Have mercy *and* compassion on us, [a]Son of David (Messiah)!" [28] When He went into the house, the blind men came up to Him, and Jesus said to them, "Do you believe [with a deep, abiding trust] that I am able to do this?" They said to Him, "Yes, Lord." [29] Then He touched their eyes, saying, "According to your faith [your trust and confidence in My power and My ability to heal] it will be done to you." [30] And their eyes were opened. And Jesus [b]sternly warned them: "See that no one knows this!"

Insight:

I wanted to use the amplified version for emphasis and sincerity of the blind men. They knew the power of Jesus to heal, they sought His mercy and compassion. Again, it was their faith that Jesus considered (according to your faith it will be done.)

Three items however are important to consider.

1. Ask for needs that you know only Jesus can provide, not if you can do them!
2. Do this all in faith in Jesus Christ believing that Jesus is always able to do anything, anywhere to anyone according to His will.
3. Continue to pray and fast so you may have His power working in you, listen for His direction and insight in all areas.

Jesus emphasis of faith in Him to do all manner of healing is extremely important.

Your Thoughts:

DAVID OVERCOMES GOLIATH

1 Samuel 17:38-51 NIV

[38] Then Saul dressed David in his own tunic. He put a coat of armor on him and a bronze helmet on his head. [39] David fastened on his sword over the tunic and tried walking around, because he was not used to them.

"I cannot go in these," he said to Saul, "because I am not used to them." So, he took them off. [40] Then he took his staff in his hand, chose five smooth stones from the stream, put them in the pouch of his shepherd's bag and, with his sling in his hand, approached the Philistine.

[41] Meanwhile, the Philistine, with his shield bearer in front of him, kept coming closer to David. [42] He looked David over and saw that he was little more than a boy, glowing with health and handsome, and he despised him. [43] He said to David, "Am I a dog, that you come at me with sticks?" And the Philistine cursed David by his gods. [44] "Come here," he said, "and I'll give your flesh to the birds and the wild animals!"

[45] David said to the Philistine, "You come against me with sword and spear and javelin, but I come against you in the name of the LORD Almighty, the God of the armies of Israel, whom you have defied. [46] This day the LORD will deliver you into my hands, and I'll strike you down and cut off your head. This very day I will give the carcasses of the Philistine army to the birds and the wild animals, and the whole world will know that there is a God in Israel. [47] All those gathered here will know that it is not by sword or spear that the LORD saves; for the battle is the LORD's, and he will give all of you into our hands."

[48] As the Philistine moved closer to attack him, David ran quickly toward the battle line to meet him. [49] Reaching into his bag and taking out a stone, he slung it and struck the Philistine on the forehead. The stone sank into his forehead, and he fell face down on the ground.

[50] So David triumphed over the Philistine with a sling and a stone; without a sword in his hand he struck down the Philistine and killed him.

[51] David ran and stood over him. He took hold of the Philistine's sword and drew it from the sheath. After he killed him, he cut off his head with the sword.

When the Philistines saw that their hero was dead, they turned and ran.

Insight:

This account of young David's victory over the giant Goliath was strongly based on David's faith in God. He was tested before as a shepherd vs 34-37 and proven faithful. God gave him much favor.

In the passage it is interesting to note that David spoke up when God was blasphemed by Goliath. God does not need defending but believers are to proclaim him always in honor and glory against all evil. God rewards the faithful who call on Him. Too many times we fear; read what Proverbs 29:25 says about this. Fearing people is a dangerous trap, but trusting the LORD means safety.

David came against Goliath in the name of the Lord Almighty 1 Samuel 17:45. David trusted God for the victory in His power.

When you are confronted with seemingly insurmountable situation and problems that is the time to exercise faith and depend on the Holy Spirit power. This is the way to do works in faith.

Faith in God must become a lifestyle for each of us. Our faith in God is built on experiencing and seeing God involved in all our life.

Contrary to human wisdom, begin praising God in all situations for this is God's will for you in Christ Jesus. 1 Thessalonians 5:18 NLT

Your Thoughts:

THE FIG TREE DRIES UP

Matthew 21:18-22 NLV

¹⁸ In the morning as He was coming back to the city, He was hungry. ¹⁹ He saw a fig tree by the side of the road and went to it. There was nothing on it but leaves. He said to the tree, "No fruit will ever grow on you again." At once the fig tree dried up. ²⁰ The followers saw it and were surprised and wondered. They said, "How did the fig tree dry up so fast?" ²¹ Jesus said to them, "For sure, I tell you this: If you have faith and do not doubt, you will not only be able to do what was done to the fig tree. You will also be able to say to this mountain, 'Move from here and be thrown into the sea,' and it will be done. ²² All things you ask for in prayer, you will receive if you have faith."

Insight:

Jesus says prayer is related to our faith. Faith is paramount (more important than anything else, supreme). Our faith in Christ must grow to see his work within us increase.

Jesus demonstrates the power of prayer in faith to show us the unlimited power we have available in each of us. We are to produce, bear fruit, that is good works.

Let us believe and not doubt when we pray in faith for something. Remember it must agree with God's word, He only gives good gifts to us in His time. Wait upon the Lord and you will be surprised how quickly some prayers are answered, and when they are answered praise the Lord and share with others what the Lord has done.

This builds your faith and others.

Your Thoughts:

JESUS CALMS THE STORM

Mark 4:35-41 NIV

³⁵ That day when evening came, he said to his disciples, "Let us go over to the other side." ³⁶ Leaving the crowd behind, they took him along, just as he was, in the boat. There were also other boats with him. ³⁷ A furious squall came up, and the waves broke over the boat, so that it was nearly swamped. ³⁸ Jesus was in the stern, sleeping on a cushion. The disciples woke him and said to him, "Teacher, don't you care if we drown?" ³⁹ He got up, rebuked the wind and said to the waves, "Quiet! Be still!" Then the wind died down and it was completely calm. ⁴⁰ He said to his disciples, "Why are you so afraid? Do you still have no faith?" ⁴¹ They were terrified and asked each other, "Who is this? Even the wind and the waves obey him!"

Insight:

Of all the people God used, blessed, did miracles signs and wonders. Faith was the common denominator among all of them. We are to live by faith in Christ.

Romans 1:17 ¹⁷ For in the gospel the righteousness of God is revealed—a righteousness that is by faith from first to last, just as it is written: "The righteous will live by faith."

There are many scriptures references identifying faith in Christ with Holy Spirit power. When you walk in faith God will show you when and where and what to do and who will be affected. Trust God.

Your Thoughts:

BLIND BARTIMAEUS RECEIVES HIS SIGHT

Mark 10:46-52 NIV

⁴⁶ Then they came to Jericho. As Jesus and his disciples, together with a large crowd, were leaving the city, a blind man, Bartimaeus (which means "son of Timaeus"), was sitting by the roadside begging. ⁴⁷ When he heard that it was Jesus of Nazareth, he began to shout, "Jesus, Son of David, have mercy on me!" ⁴⁸ Many rebuked him and told him to be quiet, but he shouted all the more, "Son of David, have mercy on me!" ⁴⁹ Jesus stopped and said, "Call him."

So they called to the blind man, "Cheer up! On your feet! He's calling you." ⁵⁰ Throwing his cloak aside, he jumped to his feet and came to Jesus. ⁵¹ "What do you want me to do for you?" Jesus asked him. The blind man said, "Rabbi, I want to see." ⁵² "Go," said Jesus, "your faith has healed you." Immediately he received his sight and followed Jesus along the road.

Insight:

Jesus heals another blind man named Bartimaeus just by speaking a word! Vs 52.

Again, Jesus always recognizes the faith one has and considers it when he heals someone. Jesus seems to never use the same method to heal or do miracles; likewise we should not use a "system" for healing. Only Jesus heals and may use you and I in different ways to accomplish it.

Can you imagine the encouragement people have when they experienced some one being healed? So is our testimony when we are healed or know of others healed. Share it!

As we are guided by the Holy Spirit, we will know how to proceed in any of our spiritual gifts. Jesus never changes but His methods can. For examples Jesus used mud, cast out demons by speaking to them, Jesus spoke a word, Peter's shadow, Paul's handkerchief, the faith of people asking for healing, etc.…

Today some ministries and people attempt to imitate the ways Jesus used to heal. Do not be caught up in that. At the same time Jesus could use these again! As your faith increases you will experience more guidance in the Holy Spirit in these matters. Jesus already knows our needs but still wants to hear about them from us.

Our bodies continue to grow physically and there is nothing we can do about it, why not purposely grow in faith every day, this we can do.

Bless His Word.

Your Thoughts:

JESUS HEALS A MAN WITH LEPROSY

Matthew 8:1-4 NIV

1 When Jesus came down from the mountainside, large crowds followed him. ² A man with leprosy came and knelt before him and said, "Lord, if you are willing, you can make me clean." ³ Jesus reached out his hand and touched the man. "I am willing," he said. "Be clean!" Immediately he was cleansed of his leprosy. ⁴ Then Jesus said to him, "See that you don't tell anyone. But go, show yourself to the priest and offer the gift Moses commanded, as a testimony to them."

Matthew 8:14-17 Jesus Heals Many others
¹⁴ When Jesus came into Peter's house, he saw Peter's mother-in-law lying in bed with a fever. ¹⁵ He touched her hand and the fever left her, and she got up and began to wait on him.

¹⁶ When evening came, many who were demon-possessed were brought to him, and he drove out the spirits with a word and healed all the sick. ¹⁷ This was to fulfill what was spoken through the prophet Isaiah: "He took up our infirmities and bore our diseases."

He says it all in John 14:11-14

¹¹ Believe me when I say that I am in the Father and the Father is in me; or at least believe on the evidence of the works themselves. ¹² Very truly I tell you, whoever believes in me will do the works I have been doing, and they will do even greater things than these, because I am going to the Father. ¹³ And I will do whatever you ask in my name, so that the Father may be glorified in the Son. ¹⁴ You may ask me for anything in my name, and I will do it.

Insight:

There is no limit on who Jesus can heal. These scriptures continue to demonstrate the many types of healing He did and still does. It is basically a matter of believing who Jesus says He is. Jesus say we will do even greater things than these! John 14:12

As you grow in faith you will still be amazed how much more we will do in the Lord's work.

Continue to practice using your faith to do more and see what God will do.

Your Thoughts:

PETER HEALS A CRIPPLE

Acts 3:16 NIV

[16]By faith in the name of Jesus, this man whom you see and know was made strong. It is Jesus' name and the faith that comes through him that has completely healed him, as you can all see.

Insight:

Read Acts 3 for the full understanding of this passage.

God always has a purpose for what He does.

After Peter heals a crippled beggar in the name of Jesus Christ of Nazareth. The whole town hears about it and comes to Peter astonished. Peter speaks to the onlookers and tells them of God's plan to send Jesus that they and their leaders have rejected. That God raised Jesus from the dead to bless them and turn them from their sinful ways.

Take time to highlight the details that stand out in the scriptures and learn these truths.

Your Thoughts:

PAUL SPOKE HEALING TO LAME MAN

Acts 14:8-10 NIV

[8] In Lystra there sat a man who was lame. He had been that way from birth and had never walked. [9] He listened to Paul as he was speaking. Paul looked directly at him, saw that he had faith to be healed [10] and called out, "Stand up on your feet!" At that, the man jumped up and began to walk.

Insight:

Here the Apostle had spiritual insight, (word of knowledge and discernment) from the Holy Spirit. He discerned the man had faith to believe for healing. We know that God can use any means to bring healing.

These are gifts of the Spirit found in 1 Corinthians 12 and 14. Believers today are to seek all the gifts of the Spirit.

This is not a matter of man's doctrine of whether all the gifts are available to the believers today. In a word, they are! Remember Hebrews 3:8.

All power is given to us as believers. It is our duty to be obedient to God's Word and Will. Since the Holy Spirit is in all believers{1Corinthians 6:19} let us use these gifts for His glory.

A study on the spiritual gifts would bring much maturity to believers and Holy Spirit power to become great witnesses for Christ.

Your Thoughts:

PAUL'S ENCOURAGEMENT

1Thessalonians 5:16-22 NIV

[16] Rejoice always, [17] pray continually, [18] give thanks in all circumstances; for this is God's will for you in Christ Jesus.

[19] Do not quench the Spirit. [20] Do not treat prophecies with contempt [21] but test them all; hold on to what is good, [22] reject every kind of evil.

Insight:

Let us began practicing our faith by always living with thankfulness in all situations. The devil wants to discourage us any time things become difficult for us. All of these instructions are for our benefit. This is one of the most demanding scriptures. Why? Because it seems so unreasonable to our human nature. How do we give thanks when things are going bad for us or around us? We cannot understand this in the natural realm because it is a spiritual principle from God's Word. Obeying and living with this concept allows the Holy Spirit to become involved in the matter(s) at hand.

Verses 16-18 are foundational for all believers since it is God's will for us. Many ask what is God's will for me? These are the answers! It is clearly defined in these scriptures.

Verses 19-22 gives more truths about the Holy Spirit using the spiritual gifts, because if you reject prophecies you in effect reject Word of Wisdom, Word of Knowledge, Tongues, Interpretation, Prophecy, Discernment (that can come in a tongue), in other words most of the spiritual gifts found in 1 Corinthians 12 and 14, could come through a prophetic word!

The spiritual gifts were given to empower the believers in everyday life and to be a witness of the power of the cross of Jesus Christ. Study the gifts and ask God to show you those He has given you and begin using them. You will also recognize some of these gifts in others.

Praise the Lord.

Your Thoughts:

APOSTLE PAUL A PRISONER

Acts 27:1-12 NIV

Acts 27:13-26

[13] When a gentle south wind began to blow, they saw their opportunity; so they weighed anchor and sailed along the shore of Crete. [14] Before very long, a wind of hurricane force, called the Northeaster, swept down from the island. [15] The ship was caught by the storm and could not head into the wind; so we gave way to it and were driven along. [16] As we passed to the lee of a small island called Cauda, we were hardly able to make the lifeboat secure, [17] so the men hoisted it aboard. Then they passed ropes under the ship itself to hold it together. Because they were afraid they would run aground on the sandbars of Syrtis, they lowered the sea anchor[b] and let the ship be driven along. [18] We took such a violent battering from the storm that the next day they began to throw the cargo overboard. [19] On the third day, they threw the ship's tackle overboard with their own hands. [20] When neither sun nor stars appeared for many days and the storm continued raging, we finally gave up all hope of being saved.

[21] After they had gone a long time without food, Paul stood up before them and said: "Men, you should have taken my advice not to sail from Crete; then you would have spared yourselves this damage and loss. [22] But now I urge you to keep up your courage, because not one of you will be lost; only the ship will be destroyed. [23] Last night an angel of the God to whom I belong and whom I serve stood beside me [24] and said, 'Do not be afraid, Paul. You must stand trial before Caesar; and God has graciously given you the lives of all who sail with you.' [25] So keep up your courage, men, for I have faith in God that it will happen just as he told me. [26] Nevertheless, we must run aground on some island."

Insight:

When God has a plan for you, He will bring it to pass no matter what storms we face in life. He has a purpose and a place for you to be. Apostle Paul experienced this when an angel of God spoke to him during the storm at sea telling him that he and all the crew would be safe. Vs 23-25. Paul had faith when God sent an angel to him, Paul responded by encouraging the crew to be encouraged.

God can use any means to communicate with you. In 1 Kings 19:12 God spoke to Elijah in a small whisper (still small voice). Believers today also must stay tuned to hearing the Lord by taking time to being still and listen. Know that God can speak to you though various means and people. They may not even be believers! Remember praying has two parts, speaking and listening.

Your Thoughts:

HOW TO INCREASE YOUR FAITH

Romans 10:14-17 NIV

14 How, then, can they call on the one they have not believed in? And how can they believe in the one of whom they have not heard? And how can they hear without someone preaching to them? 15 And how can anyone preach unless they are sent? As it is written: "How beautiful are the feet of those who bring good news!"

16 But not all the Israelites accepted the good news. For Isaiah says, "Lord, who has believed our message?" 17 Consequently, faith comes from hearing the message, and the message is heard through the word about Christ.

Romans 12:3-4 NIV Apostle Paul speaking.
3 For I say, through the grace given to me, to everyone who is among you, not to think *of himself* more highly than he ought to think, but to think soberly, as God has dealt to each one a measure of faith.

Matthew 17:20 NKJV
20 So Jesus said to them, "Because of your unbelief; for assuredly, I say to you, if you have faith as a mustard seed, you will say to this mountain, 'Move from here to there,' and it will move; and nothing will be impossible for you.

This is the Mustard seed Jesus was talking about.
Mustard trees have been found in various locations throughout the world. Even though it's one of the smallest seeds, the trees can grow up to 20 feet tall *and* 20 feet wide. The tree can grow in arid, dry climates and thrive even in clay or sandy soil. It can grow in hot, dry weather or cool, wet climates. I see the mustard seed as being symbolic of faith in that our faith can be tested in the "dry times", the most difficult of circumstances (drought, poor soil, and in clay or sandy ground). Also, even if the tree is cut down to the trunk, it can grow back again, so the analogy is that even during times of pruning, the believer can overcome and come back stronger than ever, just like the mustard tree that's been severely pruned and even if only a tiny bit of faith remains. The mustard tree is drought tolerant and if we have faith even the size of a tiny mustard seed, we too can tolerate the dry times in our lives, the difficult growing seasons of a Christian, and even when we are "planted" in poor soil we can still grow, even if we only have a small amount of faith. Incidentally, the mustard tree has many uses. The leaves can be made into, you guessed it, mustard. The tree can produce edible salts, some have used the small branches as toothbrushes, the leaves have been shown to prevent tooth decay and alleviate tooth aches. The implications of this tree are not lost in a dead and decaying world.

Insight:

We have all been given a measure of faith. Romans 12:3 NKJV Jesus said if we he faith the size of a mustard seed nothing will be impossible for you. We are to live by faith and our faith will increase as we hear the message of Christ.

Doing these will increase your faith:

Hear and receive the message of Jesus Christ by faith. Romans 10:17
Love God and people. Luke 10:27.
Walk by faith not by sight. 2 Corinthians 5:7
Praise God in all situations. 1 Thessalonians 5:18
Be encouraged by your answered prayers and those of others. John 16:24
Use the spiritual gifts you were given. 1 Corinthians 12:8-11
Use your spiritual gifts to bless others. 1 Corinthians 12:7
Develop your character to grow in the fruit of the spirit. Galatians 5:22-23
Pray and listen to the Holy Spirit that is in you. 1 Corinthians 6:19
Continue to read and study God's word for guidance, wisdom knowledge in all matters of life.
Finally, believe in all the promises of God. 2 Corinthians 1:20

Your Thoughts:

THE CENTER OF THE BIBLE

Q. What is the shortest chapter in the Bible?
A. Psalms 117

Q. What is the longest chapter in the Bible?
A. Psalms 119

Q. What chapter is in the center of the Bible?
A. Psalms 118

Fact: There are 594 chapters before Psalms 118
Fact: There are 594 chapters after Psalms 118
And these numbers add up to 1188

Q. What is the center verse in the Bible?
A. Psalms 118:8 NIV It is better to take refuge in the LORD
than to trust in humans.

Does this vs 118:8, say something significant about God's perfect will for our lives? The next time someone says they would like to find God's perfect will for their life and they want to be in the center of His will, just send them to the center of His Word.

In writing "Foot Washings", Reverend Couture hopes to provide the reader with personal guidance through deeper study of the Bible and preaching and teaching outlines to reach people with the Gospel of Jesus Christ.

Roger completed courses for his ordination in the Assemblies of God from Berean College, Springfield, MO.

Roger is now ordained with Maranatha Ministerial Fellowship International. (mmfi.org) He has been in ministry since 1982, serving as Pastor, teacher and mentor; in churches, men's groups, Teen Challenge, Bible studies. He has been on foreign mission trips sharing the Word of God. After 40 years, he continues to share his devotions in prisons. His emphasis is always to present Jesus Christ, as declared in the Scriptures, as the Savior and Lord of his life.

Before Roger received Jesus Christ as his Savior. he was a religious man, attending church, doing good deeds but not having or knowing the power of God through Jesus Christ in his life. He received Christ by faith in 1981 and hit the ground running according to his wife.

He and Marjorie have been married 60 years. They are blessed with 4 children, 11 grandchildren, and as of this writing, 14 great-grandchildren.

Roger A. Couture
servantshousemin@gmail.com
www.footwashings.com

Printed in the United States
By Bookmasters